Conversations with Madeleine Milhaud

By the same author

Debussy Remembered
Ravel Remembered

Conversations with Madeleine Milhaud

Roger Nichols

faber and faber

First published in 1996
by Faber and Faber Limited
3 Queen Square London WC1N 3AU

Typeset by Faber and Faber Ltd
Printed in England by Clays Ltd, St Ives plc

© Roger Nichols, 1996
Illustrations © Madeleine Milhaud, 1996

Roger Nichols is hereby identified as author of this
work in accordance with Section 77 of the Copyright,
Designs and Patents Act 1988

A CIP record for this book
is available from the British Library

ISBN 0–571–16055–7

10 9 8 7 6 5 4 3 2 1

Foreword

This book is based on a series of conversations between Mme Milhaud and myself which I taped in her Paris apartment over a happy week in April 1991. Since then, she has revised the text extensively – one story would remind her of another, or we would find that Milhaud himself had dealt with such and such a topic in his memoirs, or a new ordering of material would be adopted to bring some particular point better into focus. And if at times Mme Milhaud's English seems not to be quite in the current mode, that is not (as she, in her modesty, is always claiming) the result of linguistic incompetence, but of the fact that she learned her English before the First World War, when the nuance still held sway.

Our joint acknowledgements go, firstly, but without too many thanks, to Mme Milhaud's devoted companion Mitsou, who chewed cables, trod on rewind buttons, sat on interview notes and generally did his best to make the whole project as difficult as possible (I hope the photograph on page 103 is some kind of sop); and secondly, with heartfelt thanks, to Dr Jeremy Drake, who kept an editorial eye on the text from its earliest stages and who gave unstintingly of his time in preparing it finally for press.

My own personal thanks go to Mme Milhaud herself, for her patience and understanding during the rather long gestation of the book, for her most generous hospitality, and for allowing me to share, albeit vicariously, in her extraordinary life.

Roger Nichols
Kington, January 1996

1. Madeleine Milhaud, 1935

Roger Nichols: There's a plaque on the outside of this house on the Boulevard de Clichy saying 'Darius Milhaud lived here 1923–1974'. That's a long time to stay in one place. I wonder, why this particular *quartier*?

Madeleine Milhaud: Well, I suppose he liked it! Montmartre has always attracted artists: so many painters until World War I, and musicians, actors, composers. Honegger, Sauguet and Wiéner lived close by. But it is not the place it was when Darius moved to Paris in 1910. At that time he was looking for a flat not too far from the Conservatoire. He rented one in a very small, charming street then called the rue Gaillard, where he stayed for nearly fifteen years. Darius was my father's nephew and used to visit us a few times a year as we lived nearby.

What are your first memories of him, before he came to live in Paris?

He was ten years older than me. To be sincere, I don't have any memories of him, but I decided he had some of me! When he was taken by his mother to visit his aunt, he saw a delightfully pretty little baby girl in a cradle and decided then and there that she would be his wife. It's a charming story, but an absolute lie!

Your father came from Aix-en-Provence?

My father had left Aix to study law in Paris and had stayed on. So, for as long as my grandmother was alive, we only went to Aix for a few days every year at Easter. The family in Aix was a real provincial family, nobody had ever left the town. My father was the only renegade! He was rather ambitious, like a hero in a novel of Balzac. He was attracted by works of art, luxury and politics. He had definite ideas about hygiene, food and diet. I realized when I was older that the arrival of the Parisians was regarded as something funny that the Aix family looked forward to each year – plus the fact that my mother loved to dress me in a most elegant manner. She had a passion for English fashions, and the material would come from Liberty's. My English governess used to pick up dead leaves to try to find the right shade of velvet material to dress up the little monkey – the monkey was myself! – with a sort of brownish colour which Liberty's would approve

2. Madeleine aged 8

of. I hated it but the people of Aix thought it was funny!

As for Darius, his life followed a regular rhythm. He came back to Paris in late September for the Conservatoire and returned to Aix for Christmas and Easter, as well as for summer of course. In fact he spent all his summers in Aix until 1940 – as we did when we were married!!

Although he could work anywhere, Aix was more conducive to work because it was the atmosphere he knew and loved. Nature had great importance for Darius and it was not only the fragrance of the flowers or the trees; it was the landscape, the same landscape that had had such a strong effect on Cézanne, and it's not surprising that Milhaud's First String Quartet is dedicated to the artist's memory. He was also very much influenced by anything he heard. Birds, insects had great, great importance for him. You can see why so many of his works are pastorales.

Darius was always very receptive to noise. He has described in his book the noises that he heard from his bedroom when the workers were operating the machines, and also the different types of rhythm. As for the insects, you never know what they are, they just appear at night and disappear – very mysterious! Of course the summum of that is *L'Homme et son Désir*, because there you have the sounds of a whole forest, the tropical forest of Brazil that had so impressed him. But it's possible he would never have written *L'Homme et son Désir* if he had not already been impregnated by this influence.

There were other reasons for Milhaud to be attracted to Aix. He had a very deep affection for his parents and especially for his mother. She was of Italian origin and was passionately devoted to her only son. He was the only thing that mattered to her! She had been a rather severe mother, inculcating in him a sense of duty which he retained all his life. Yet, as Milhaud did not have a very strong constitution, she relieved him of any needless tasks. If he had been punished by his teacher and had to write out fifty times 'I am a naughty little boy', she would do the lines for him so that he could spend time practising the violin. She was well aware of his musical qualities and was full of ambition for him. She wanted him to become a virtuoso. Later on she became very highly strung – Darius and his father were always afraid of aggravating her anxieties. In the end that produced a very strange atmosphere in the house. During the two

3

3. Milhaud with his parents at L'Enclos, Aix-en-Provence, 1910

months of summer holidays Milhaud only rarely dared take two or three days off and go away somewhere with a friend. He did it once or twice with Léo Latil when they went together to Les-Saintes-Maries-de-la-Mer, but it was difficult.

And his father?

He was a silent, extremely patient man, very sensitive, but hiding his feelings and his thoughts. When I lived with Darius I was very touched by his qualities. Friends used only to talk about Darius's mother. I always found that rather unjust. Milhaud's friends were impressed by his father's kindness and hospitality during their visits. He was an excellent pianist and would accompany Milhaud when he was young, as he did for Milhaud's first public concert – which he gave at the age of eight.

What was your life like in Aix?

Very simple. Darius would work all day, but three times a week we went to the market where people were selling antiques of various sorts. Nearly every day, towards the end of the afternoon, Darius with his friend Armand Lunel would be outside one of those shops run by dealers who go out into the countryside looking for old furniture, old vases and so on – in those days there were vast amounts of things to be found in attics and cellars. They both had a veritable passion for 'hunting' antiques. Then, we would walk for an hour or two in that countryside around Aix that is still so particularly attractive. Aix at that time was a town of silence, a sort of Sleeping Beauty. As in most provincial towns there were no cars of course.

What were the people like in Aix?

The people of Aix had very regular habits. My father-in-law used to take a carriage every day in summer from his office to his country house, L'Enclos, about a mile away. One day Darius and I were in the Café des Deux Garçons at the end of the main avenue, the Cours Mirabeau, when the waiter said 'It's twelve o'clock. Monsieur Milhaud is going past'. One can't believe that life was once like that, but it was!

It was the custom in certain families to spend the summer months in the country, and in some cases these residences were in fact very close to town, as L'Enclos was. Milhaud was greatly attached to this house and when he returned from America after the war to find that L'Enclos had been plundered by the Germans, it was such a shock that he decided he would never ever live in it again. I always respected his decisions, and after all the house did belong to him, but it could have been saved, although the surrounding meadows had gone and huge blocks of flats had been built up around it.

Would you say there was any detectable difference between the works he wrote here and those he wrote in Paris?

If there was any difference I think it lay in the fact that he could work in Aix with greater tranquillity. In Paris he was constantly being disturbed. In the past you would write to someone for an appointment, but with the telephone people got into the habit of calling for anything and everything. It was sometimes quite unbearable. Another difference lay simply in the matter of opportunity. From 1932 until the war Milhaud composed twenty or so scores of incidental music and several for the movies. If he had lived in Aix he probably would not have been asked so much, but there was the question of earning a living!

Did Milhaud find it hard to talk to people who weren't at all musical?

Certainly not, otherwise he would never have been so intimate with Lunel and Latil. And he enjoyed visiting our cousin Gabrielle Léon, whose husband Xavier was a philosopher who had founded an important magazine, *La Revue de Métaphysique et Morale*. Xavier was friendly with Bergson, Alain and many other philosophers as well as with artists. Cortot, Thibaud, Rabaud came to see him frequently. I often helped my cousin serve tea, and I shall never forget the presence of a Scottish philosopher in full kilt and beret!

As far as my parents were concerned Darius and they had no common interests, and my brother had quite different literary tastes, preferring Renan and Anatole France to Jammes and Claudel. Moreover, he was an absolute stranger to music – it annoyed him even, and when I used to practise the piano he would offer me money to stop playing. On the other hand he had a great literary gift and wrote a novel that was published.

My brother was seven when I was born, and my mother was so happy to have a little girl that she completely turned away from her son. He suffered greatly because of this, though he never bore me a grudge, which is amazing. He even attached himself to me with love and admiration. In fact I acted as his mother, though I was seven years younger, and he acted as my father, being an important part of my education – at least, it was he who told me about certain things! My mother kept telling me that babies were born in cabbages. Thanks to Étienne I learned that these things happened in a perfectly normal and simple way. Obviously this complicity created a rather special atmosphere and Milhaud, who was more puritan than we were, was a little wary of our relationship.

Did you ever hear him play the violin?

Never! I just knew he was taking exams, and that his parents were very proud of him, that is, until the day he decided to end his violin lessons and devote himself to composition.

How did his parents react?

His mother was dismayed, but she had to accept the situation. Her son was going to be a composer. In fact he already was one, as he had by then written several works – even an opera, *Les Saintes Maries de la Mer*. Yet his violin studies were very beneficial. He was in his violin teacher's string quartet when he was twelve and this developed his taste for chamber music, so it's not at all surprising that when Cocteau asked him in 1919 to contribute to his revue *Le Coq*, Milhaud defended chamber music, which at that time was not quite *à la mode* with young composers. It was then that he forecast 'I shall write eighteen quartets' – and he had already written four and was working on a fifth. Naturally this profession of faith was misinterpreted in the sense merely of 'Haha! one more than Beethoven!'. Was it a joke? It's possible, but it did also correspond to something serious and important for Milhaud.

Who did he study the violin with at the Conservatoire?

With an excellent musician, Berthelier. They became very close. Darius even presented me to his wife when I wanted to do some chamber music.

What did Milhaud think of his other teachers?

Darius thought that Paul Dukas, who took the orchestral classes, was a better composer than teacher!

Was Milhaud a good student?

Extremely serious. He did what he was supposed to do, though not always with pleasure. He hated harmony, for instance, and it was a great burden for him to study it in the way it was taught. He was convinced that prolonged harmony studies would make him lose his personality. He tried in vain to show his music to his teacher Xavier Leroux, but Leroux did not want to spend time on such a mediocre student. Darius insisted and was at length able to play him his Violin Sonata. He had hardly finished the first movement when Leroux said to him, 'Why waste your time in this class? You have your own language, go away!'. This entailed a fairly serious decision, so he asked the advice of Henri Rabaud – a friend of Xavier Léon – who gave him a letter of recommendation for André Gedalge. The visit to Gedalge made a strong impression on Darius for he at once asked, 'Do you want to win prizes or learn your trade?'. According to the pupil's reply he would accept him in his own class or not. Naturally Darius wanted to learn technique and felt that he had been saved and would be in good hands. Gedalge was indeed an exceptional teacher. He took such a close interest in his pupils, that he offered to give orchestration classes to Darius and his classmates Wiéner, Ibert and Honegger without asking for payment – for his own pleasure!

Were Milhaud's friends exclusively musicians?

Certainly not. His friendships in Aix show that. Latil was a poet and Lunel a writer.

Léo Latil was the son of the Milhaud family doctor. He had lost his mother when still very young and I think he suffered greatly from it. Léo took violin lessons with Milhaud's teacher M. Bruguier, but he wasn't really a musician. He was a very sensitive, highly strung, fragile young man. He wrote poetry, but loved music in his way. He admired Milhaud and held him in great affection. He thought he was the only person who could understand him. Léo was a mystic, and would probably have been a priest if he had not been killed in the war in 1915.

This friendship might perhaps have become a little morbid had Darius not got to know Armand Lunel at the lycée. Armand was more positive and had a fertile imagination as well as a perfect knowledge of the history of Provence. His family had the same Jewish origin as ours. He knew everything about our ancestors who had lived in the Comtat Venaissin under the domination of the popes for centuries. It was Armand who was Darius's first collaborator. He wrote vast poems inspired by Persia, India, Greece, etc., that Darius set to music. All that was burnt in due course. When Lunel and Darius left school in Aix they went to Paris, Darius to the Conservatoire, Lunel to study philosophy at the École Normale. The two would meet every Sunday, and sometimes also during the week. They were fascinated by painting and went to all the exhibitions. They of course attended concerts and every Sunday morning they would go to the flea market. Léo felt rather isolated after Darius's departure, but they wrote to each other regularly. One day Léo wrote to Darius to suggest he read a play by Francis Jammes which had just been published in a magazine: *La Brebis Égarée*. The play greatly touched Darius who immediately wanted to turn it into an opera. But how could he get the author's permission? There was in Aix a charming lady musician who knew Jammes; she was a remarkable photographer and had made a portrait of him. She undertook to convey Darius's wishes to Jammes. It is extraordinary that a famous poet should agree to an unknown music student writing an opera on one of his works, but he did, and Darius at once set to work. Four years later *La Brebis Égarée* was finished!

He went to see Jammes when he had completed the composition of the first act. Léo went with him. They were warmly received by the poet and his wife. Jammes did not seem displeased with the music, which encouraged Darius to play him some songs he written with texts from *La Connaissance de l'Est* by Claudel. Jammes at once proposed writing to Claudel about him and so, a few weeks later, Claudel, who was then French Consul in Frankfurt, announced that he would be coming to see Darius. Darius could not imagine that the writer he admired so much would pay him a visit – but that marked the start of a collaboration which lasted until 1967.

I can understand Milhaud's admiration for Claudel, but I wonder why Milhaud and his friends were attracted by Jammes?

Milhaud found a simplicity in Jammes' poetry and a homely character which were a reaction against the poetry of the Symbolists, but it was Claudel's prophet-like lyricism that was the closest to Darius.

The very first day they met their understanding was total. After Claudel heard the *Connaissance de l'Est* he spoke of Aeschylus's Oresteian trilogy which he was translating. He mentioned the problem of certain spoken parts and how they could be illustrated by music. Darius never let himself be over-influenced by Claudel and at once expressed his own ideas on the subject. He hated the sound of the spoken word with music in the background, which is what gave him the idea, when he was composing *Les Choéphores*, of having the text in certain passages rhythmically recited while the chorus spoke syllables and uttered sounds in set rhythms backed up by the percussion. Claudel was greatly interested in Milhaud's ideas and, as he was very impulsive, Darius had the impression that he was ready to give him all his works to set to music! A few months later Claudel invited Darius to join him in Hellerau where *L'Annonce Faite à Marie* was being staged in the new theatre. Milhaud attended the rehearsals with much interest and even helped by fixing some bell chimes that were in the play. In between rehearsals he went on long walks with Claudel who told him about his youth, the painful crises he had been through and his sister's illness which was preoccupying him.

It was the first time that Milhaud made friends with a creator of genius who had had to live with ordinary human sufferings. These confidences were quite different from those of his friends in Aix.

Did you ever meet Lunel and Latil at that time?

Not at that time. But I did meet Léo once at the start of the war, in Aix. He looked at me with a grave face and said, 'Hello Madeleine Milhaud, cousin of Darius'. I shall never forget the intensity and the gentleness of his look. The next day he rejoined his regiment and was killed in May 1915.

Did you go often to Aix?

No, not at all since the death of my grandmother. But at the beginning of the war, as my father was fearful of a German offensive, he insisted that my mother and I leave Paris. That was how we arrived in Aix in early August.

What was the atmosphere like then?

The south of France hardly bothered at all about what was happening in the north. But we very soon had bad news with the death of relatives and friends, and freedom from care took a hard dose of reality.

Darius had been rejected for army service because of his health, so he settled at L'Enclos with his parents. It was during this stay that we became comrades. We often went for walks together. Since I could sight-read easily he enjoyed playing difficult works with me on the piano, such as *The Rite of Spring* and *Petrushka*. I flattered his gourmandise by making strange little delicacies. Miss Thomassin, my drama teacher, had joined us at Aix and she forced me to learn patriotic poems of doubtful quality. This exasperated Darius who tried in vain to suggest I recite Claudel or Jammes instead.

We returned to Paris after the Battle of the Marne in 1915. At that time we were living very close to Darius. My mother and I occupied two ground-floor rooms. Whenever Darius came back from the Conservatoire he would tap on the window so we could chat a while together. There were often air-raid alerts in the evening; Darius had got into the habit of coming to join us. They were very relaxed, sometimes even jolly meetings.

Then my parents moved for a while to the Paris region and I rarely saw Darius. He had offered his services to the Foyer Franco-Belge. This was a charity that helped refugees find housing and work, and Darius organized concerts for the Foyer in order to raise funds. André Gide was also closely involved in the charity. Darius knew him slightly as he had written a suite for voice and piano, *Alissa*, which set extracts of Gide's novel *La Porte Étroite*. Gide went to see Darius a few times. He was particularly attracted to the music of Chopin and had very interesting ideas on its interpretation. It was as a souvenir of these meetings that Darius dedicated his Second Violin Sonata to André Gide and that at the end of the second movement he introduced a few bars of Chopin's *Barcarolle*.

Léo's death at the front in May 1915 had a dramatic effect on Darius, but he threw himself into his work for the Foyer with even greater zeal, and then moved to the propaganda service of the Foreign Ministry.

All this work did not prevent him from composing. Haunted by

Léo's memory, he wrote a third string quartet at the end of which he introduced a soprano singing part of Léo's private diary. He continued to organize concerts and sometimes programmed works by a composer he much admired, Albéric Magnard, who had been killed by the Germans. Magnard's vigour and sense of the grandeur of his art had contributed to the chasing away of Impressionist magic.

And yet he liked Debussy's music!

Ever since Darius had first played through the quartet he loved all of Debussy's works unreservedly.

Did Milhaud know Debussy personally?

He only met him once, in 1915, when the publisher Durand wanted to have the Sonata for flute, viola and harp played and asked Darius to take the viola part. So Darius went to see Debussy to check the tempi. He was already very ill but still played his sonata a couple of times. Milhaud was very impressed and left without mentioning that he was a composer, even though he had just finished *Les Choéphores*.

I saw Debussy several times. The first was when I heard him play the piano; he was accompanying Jane Bathori who was singing the *Chansons de Bilitis*. His touch was quite incomparable – warm, intimate and profound all at once. His daughter was following the same piano lessons as myself with Marguerite Long. Debussy sometimes came to pick her up, and then . . . I played one of his *Arabesques* at the end-of-year audition – in his presence. I don't suppose he was greatly impressed, but I was certainly aware he was there! When I learnt of his death I wanted to go to his funeral, but at that moment 'Big Bertha', the long-distance cannon, was in action several times a day and my mother forbade me to go out. regretted it all the more when I learnt that so few people were there

Was Milhaud influenced by Debussy?

Yes, in the prosody of *La Brebis Égarée* and perhaps in a few early works which were destroyed. On the other hand his frequenting of

12

Koechlin was more important for Darius. He proved that by dedicating *Les Choéphores* to him. When Darius was studying Koechlin's Viola Sonata, at the composer's request, he was so enthusiastic that he wrote to Koechlin to say how much he admired it and that he regretted not having enough money to organize concerts so people could hear his music.

Koechlin's behaviour was always unpredictable. One summer he stopped at Aix to spend a few days with Darius. He left some beehives at the station, intending to take them on to his property in Normandy. When he arrived at L'Enclos, he refused to occupy the room that had been prepared for him, deciding instead to sleep in his hammock in the garden – in spite of the bad weather! The next morning the station master called: the bees were all over the station and nobody dared go in. Koechlin left right away! He had a refreshing naïvety and was in fact a delightful human being, quite unlike anyone else. Darius had met Koechlin before leaving for Brazil. They met when he got back and were thereafter constantly in touch.

When did Milhaud leave for Brazil?

In December 1917, when Claudel was appointed French Minister. He proposed that Darius accompany him. This was providential for Darius as he badly needed a break from his family, his habits. His bad health had prevented him from being called up. He took Léo's poems with him and had them published in Rio.

What was he supposed to do out there?

In those days there were no such things as cultural attachés, so he went to Brazil as Claudel's secretary in charge of propaganda for the allied cause. He translated the coded messages, he helped Claudel organize receptions, and accompanied him on all his travels, which gave him the opportunity of making some magnificent trips. He also organized concerts and lectures in aid of the English and French Red Cross. Despite all this he found time to compose and to continue his research into polytonality.

13

What about Claudel?

He had a very precise way of living. He attended the first mass every day, then he worked for himself. At a certain time his own work would be finished for the day and so he turned to his diplomatic duties. This great poet was very much interested in economic and financial matters. At the end of the day Claudel went for a walk, sometimes asking Darius to accompany him. Darius was attracted most of all by the virgin forest. Rio had its own particular charm which he conjured up in the *Saudades do Brasil*, but it was in the forest that Darius rediscovered the emotion he had felt at night at L'Enclos when he heard the noise of the insects. In Brazil it was just as mysterious but more violent.

Nijinsky was in Rio at that time. Claudel had been greatly impressed by his dancing, and at once conceived a ballet project for him and took him into the forest so he could understand what Darius and he felt. Alas, shortly afterwards Nijinsky's health put an end to his career for good.

Despite this Claudel and Darius carried on with their project, which became *L'Homme et son Désir*.

4. *L'Homme et son Désir*, Ballets Suédois, 1921; décor by Audrey Parr

know that Messiaen attended the first performance as a boy of twelve and was deeply influenced by the use of various simultaneous levels on the stage and in the orchestra. What did the levels symbolize?

There are three stage levels and four groups in the orchestra, including the singers. The stage levels represent the hours and the passage of time; below that there is the moon and its reflection in the water; on the third level is the Man, led by two identical veiled shapes, two women in fact – one is 'Image' the other 'Desire', one is 'Memory', the other 'Illusion'. The Man is suddenly surrounded by all the insects and animals of the forest until one of the women – THE woman – appears and drags him away with her.

Did Claudel have a great influence on Milhaud?

I would answer yes and no! No, because Darius did not always accept Claudel's suggestions. Yes, because there was a close connection between the verbal rhythms of Claudel's texts and the music of Milhaud. But that Claudelian sweep penetrated into Darius and gave him strength. Claudel was a unique collaborator. He always agreed to provide Darius with a text when he needed one. Conversely when Claudel wanted him to write the incidental music for Jean-Louis Barrault's stage production of *Christophe Colomb*, Milhaud agreed to do it, though it was very painful for him: in his opera he had been able to treat the same text quite freely, but in writing incidental music he was obliged to please the public and to satisfy the demands of the stage producer.

For how long were Claudel and Milhaud in Brazil?

Until the end of the war.

Did Milhaud write to you?

I sent him a card once and he answered, 'Your spelling is not good', so I did not write a second time!

15

What were your activities at this time?

I was finishing my studies and following chamber-music classes.
regularly attended the Saturday morning rehearsals of Gabrie
Pierné. That was my initiation into classical and contemporary
music. I used to read a lot – I still do – and had a reader's subscrip
tion to Adrienne Monnier's bookshop, where very famous writer
would meet regularly. What a stroke of good fortune for a seven
teen-year-old student to meet Fargues, Valéry, Larbaud, Joyce and
others! I also had a subscription with Adrienne's friend Sylvia
Beach, who had her own bookshop on the opposite pavement. This
was Shakespeare and Co., where I met all the Anglo-Saxon writer
who were staying in Paris. It was thanks to these two bookseller
that *Ulysses* was translated into French. Adrienne organized sev
eral musical seasons in her bookshop. I remember Satie accompa
nying his own *Socrate*, and the first performance of *Alissa* took
place there when Milhaud got back from Brazil.

What was your relationship with him then?

I felt right away that he had changed, and he also gave me the
impression that he was not adapted to the youthful excitement o
that post-war period, that he was not at ease with it. I imagined tha

5. Darius and Madeleine at the Montmartre fair, 1923

a Damady en toute affection

6. Darius and Madeleine on their wedding day, 1925

f I could strike up a friendship with him it could perhaps be help-
ul, and that's how it began! I couldn't tell you exactly when I fell
n love with Darius or when he realized he needed his little cousin.
Darius was a music critic then and we very often went to concerts
ogether. I always made a point of giving him my opinion straight
way after listening to a piece so as not to be influenced by him!

When did you hear his music for the first time?

cannot remember whether it was the music of his First Symphonic
Suite that so struck me or the fact that I lost a little fur wrap! That
vas in May 1914. All the same I could not then imagine that I would
be present with Darius at all the first performances of his works.

**Milhaud's most important première after the war was that of *Les
Choéphores*, I think?**

Certainly. I did not know the work, and Milhaud suggested I attend
he last rehearsal. They played the movements for orchestra and
chorus first and kept the percussion sections for the end, so the
orchestra could be allowed to go. I overheard Darius say '*on répète
a batterie*' – 'we're going to rehearse the percussion'. I thought he

7. Milhaud with Jane Bathori, Paris, 1958

had said *patrie* – motherland – instead of *batterie*, so I left! Yo
must know that young people were so fed up with the war, and
just could not bear listening to some patriotic work. At the concer
in the evening of course I realized what I had missed.

How was it received?

It had a great success and the scene that I had missed in the morn
ing had to be played a second time. The orchestra was conducte
by Félix Delgrange, though there was not enough money to pay fo
all the seventeen percussionists needed in the Exhortation scene, s
some of Darius's friends were roped in: Honegger, Cocteau, Auri
Poulenc and Lucien Daudet.

Jane Bathori had the roles of Elektra and the reciter. She wa
generous enough to find and rehearse the singers without pay
ment. She was an astonishing woman. Though a singer of Debuss
and Ravel, she was always keen on promoting new works. He
association with the Vieux Colombier Theatre came abou
because Jacques Copeau, the owner, was sent on a mission to Ne

York during World War I and asked her to run his theatre in his absence. She organized concerts, put on stage works, and was surrounded by young composers, especially Honegger, Auric, Poulenc, Roland Manuel and Ibert, under the benevolent eye of Satie. Perhaps this was the real origin of Les Six! Darius already knew these composers, so when he returned from Brazil he easily renewed contact with them. They would see each other often at this time and would go to concerts together. There were a lot of concerts then as so many musicians and conductors were interested in the new developments, and there was this series of chamber music concerts in a painter's studio in Montmartre. Very uncomfortable! But in those days the more uncomfortable a place was the better

8. 'Les Six', 1931

the snobs liked it. They had the impression they were discoverin
Art, so it was all right!

One day there was a programme containing Darius's Fourt
String Quartet and works by another five composers. Henri Colle
who, I have to say, had often been to these concerts before, wrot
that article called 'The Five Russians and the Six Frenchmen', no
that many people could say who the fifth Russian was, or the sixt
Frenchman – and she was a woman anyway! In fact they were a
very embarrassed and said, 'What are we going to do?' Finally the
thought, 'Well, perhaps it will be useful if we give concerts togethe
– the label could help.' But they all knew they were different fror
one another and had no kind of aesthetic in common – and the
didn't have the slightest intention of changing. But anyway, the
became Les Six, though I am sure that none of them dreamt tha
people would still be talking about it fifty years later.

Wasn't Cocteau the moving spirit in all that?

Naturally Cocteau saw the possibility of having an influence on som
of them, but he couldn't have any influence on Milhaud or Honegge
because both of them were already composing by 1914 and each c
them had his distinctive style. I suppose the spirit of the twenties,
there was such a thing, was closer to Auric and Poulenc than t
Milhaud and Honegger. The latter never cultivated that spirit c
impertinence which seems typical of the time. Darius's *Le Boeuf su
le Toit*, for example – as opposed to Cocteau's ballet – was not in th
spirit of the twenties: it was a reminiscence of a country that he love
– which is not at all the same thing. He had already written shor
symphonies of four minutes each in Brazil, before the fashion of shor
pieces arrived in the twenties. I must insist on that point.

What were they like?

Germaine was delightful – friendly, enthusiastic, disinterested. Sh
was well aware that she was the only woman in the group, but sh
never lost her essentially feminine qualities: elegance, lightness c
touch, wit. Honegger and Darius had been close friends at th
Conservatoire. Although Arthur was attached to and influenced b

German music, their differing tastes never came between them. They had both composed important works before Collet's famous article appeared. This was not the case with the others, though Auric had always been remarkably precocious. He had been to see Darius to play him some of his music when he was fourteen. His culture and vivacity were exceptional, and very different from the various qualities of Francis, who was closer to Chabrier in spirit. Nobody could handle buffoonery quite like him! When inspired by sacred or secular subjects he had a language and a sense of rhythm that was utterly personal. He had what we call in French *truculence*, but this is not what the English word truculence means. I'm referring to his Rabelaisian side – or Chaucerian or Falstaffian if you like!

Durey was the oldest member of the group, and had been a good friend of Cocteau before the twenties. However he could not adapt to the spirit of *Les Mariés de la Tour Eiffel* which really symbolized the mood of the twenties, and he decided not to participate in what was otherwise a joint project. And you may notice that the first picture of Les Six on the Eiffel Tower after a rehearsal of the play is without Durey.

When you say it symbolized the mood of the twenties, what do you mean?

It was a manifestation, I wouldn't say of wickedness, but of the impertinence of Cocteau and his collaborators. And in that one must include his text which, for that time, was astonishing – very daring, really. Just two years after the end of the war, when the lion says, '*Je voudrais rendre le général*' ('I want to give up, or bring up, the general' – whom he has just swallowed), the answer comes back, '*Il saura bien se rendre lui-même*' ('He'll be quite capable of giving himself up on his own'). The audience just had to take it. And the whole work was in the same style.

Durey reappeared after a few years having realized that his friends were not after all beneath consideration. They decided they would have a picture taken of themselves every ten years, and only one is missing on account of the war. The last one was taken shortly before Arthur's death. Cocteau is sitting at the piano and 'his' musicians are watching him! These photos were always taken at Darius's flat, following the tradition.

What tradition?

It was at Darius's that the group had been in the habit of meeting in 1919 – Darius was the only one to have a flat that was large enough. Every Saturday the musicians and their friends spent the whole evening together. Cocktails, dinner, circus or music hall, and then they would go back to Darius's – the evenings would carry on late into the night during which poetry and music would flow. Thus it was that Auric and Darius played *Le Boeuf sur le Toit* as a piano duet for the first time.

Where did the curious title come from?

It's the name of a song that Darius had heard in Rio during the *carnaval*. He was fascinated by the rhythms of Brazilian popular music and back in Paris he put together some tangos, maxixes, sambas and so on and composed *Le Boeuf*. He had a great admiration for the films of Charlie Chaplin and thought his music could illustrate them, though he had no one film in mind. In any event Cocteau dissuaded him from this idea and suggested they make a spectacle of it instead. Although the background would be typically Brazilian tunes, he envisaged the action taking place in New York during Prohibition, and in parallel with these unbridled rhythms he conceived a production in slow-motion, as if in a film with the speed deliberately reduced. He had in mind that this ballet would be performed by the extremely talented clowns the Fratellini Brothers, so he engaged them, and also a dwarf who was part of the Médrano Circus. Unfortunately the painter Fauconnet who was to work on the show died suddenly, but Raoul Dufy agreed to paint the sets and make the huge masks that Cocteau had imagined. The programme included *Trois Petites Pièces Montées* that Satie had specially composed, *Adieu New York* by Auric and Poulenc's *Cocardes*. The success of *Le Boeuf* led to the impression that Darius was a lightweight composer who wanted easy success and at the same time liked to scandalize the public with wrong notes!

A year after the first performance Darius went to London for a performance of *Le Boeuf* at the Coliseum.

What was Cocteau like?

Jean was sensitive, affectionate – generous, faithful – very attached to his friends. When after a couple of years the Saturday evening get-togethers attracted fewer 'Saturdayites', Jean was upset. There are letters of Jean to Darius in which he writes 'the meetings must go on'. Cocteau was not only a poet and playwright and painter, he was also a producer. In fact he was everything – and he was everywhere. He liked to be in charge of everything, and generally was at that time: if he wasn't doing everything, he didn't think he was doing anything. He was the life spirit of so many things. And then I must add, he was a sort of magician. He could transform anything – some old broken object became a work of art. There was a good example of that in the case of his adaptation of Sophocles' *Antigone*. Jean was attending the rehearsals in the Théâtre de l'Atelier. The actress playing the part of Antigone was not very good, and Jean had noticed another young woman. She was Rumanian and didn't speak a word of French, but she was the incarnation of Antigone as

9. *Le Boeuf sur le Toit*, with décor by Raoul Dufy, 1920

Jean had imagined her. So he set her to work to learn the part of Antigone by speaking slowly and separating the syllables. This worked until the rehearsals with the other actors. Then it was that Jean made everyone speak in this particular way. The effect was gripping. This special diction lent a wild, barbaric character to the play. You can see how much of a magician he was!

Well, to get back to those Saturday evenings chez Darius: they had in fact become rather boring for some people, rather like family dinners! It was Jean Wiéner who saved the situation. Wiéner had followed Gedalge's classes at the same time as Darius. They lost track of each other during the war, and when Darius saw him again he was earning a living by playing American syncopated music in the Bar Gaya. So, they all moved to the Bar Gaya, but after a while it became too small, so the owner rented another place and asked Jean Wiéner to obtain Darius's authorization to use the name of 'Le Boeuf sur le Toit' for the bar. Darius was much amused at the idea and went to see Cocteau: 'I've brought you a bar!' he said. In this way the Saturday evenings were saved. The 'Saturdayites' could go whenever they liked. Jean Wiéner and Clément Doucet played two pianos there regularly. Bach jostled with American tunesmiths. Jean went on to make syncopated music known throughout the world, but this activity was not enough for him. He became a patron and a concert organizer. I must stress the fact that, apart from him, I have never come across a composer, with practically no money and with two children to bring up, who was also a Maecenas.

Just how did he do it?

From a love of music! He called his concerts 'Salad Concerts', because he wanted to mix all sorts of genres. He had Billy Arnold's jazz band in his first concert and later programmed world premières of works by Stravinsky, as well as those piano rolls Igor had made of some of his own pieces. There was music by Ravel, Satie, Bartók, Milhaud's *Cantate de l'Enfant Prodigue* and also works by composers from central Europe which had been banned in France during the war, including Webern, Berg and Schönberg. It was Milhaud who conducted the French première of *Pierrot Lunaire*. Marya Freund agreed to be the soloist and even wrote a French translation. There were twenty-five rehearsals, and *Pierrot* had such a success that it was reprogrammed twice.

Were you present at these performances of *Pierrot*?

Yes I was.

How would you characterize Milhaud's interpretation of a work which seems so far removed from his own sound world?

I could only echo what Darius himself says. He brought out the lyrical element in the work, of which there is more than one might think. I might point out that Darius was also responsible for the

10. *From left to right:* Henri Cliquet Pleyel, Jean Wiéner, Milhaud, 1920s

British and the Belgian premières of *Pierrot*. He conducted it in London with Dorothy Moulton, the wife of Robert Mayer. I remember that the Brussels performance gave the Queen a fit of giggles!

Certainly there is a gulf between the styles of the two composers, but I think it is in part this almost absolute difference that attracted Darius to Schönberg's music, even right from the start when he first discovered the piano pieces opus 11 when at the Conservatoire. These pieces were so utterly different from his beloved *Pelléas* or *Boris Godunov*. What interested him above all was the freedom with which tonality was treated even though, as he said, the path which led to the absence of tonality was not for him.

Did Milhaud know Schönberg at the time of the *Pierrot* performances?

No. But afterwards, in 1922, Poulenc and Milhaud wanted to meet the Austrians, so they went to Vienna with Marya Freund. They had hardly arrived when Alma Mahler invited them to her house. She was very interested to learn that Milhaud had conducted *Pierrot* several times and she suggested to Schönberg a double performance of his work, Schönberg with his favourite interpreter Erika Wagner, who was in Vienna at the time, and Milhaud with his: Marya Freund. I can well imagine it must have been an exciting experience! Afterwards Schönberg invited Poulenc and Milhaud to Mödling in the environs of Vienna. He talked to them about his music. This was, don't forget, in 1922, the year before Schönberg published his first serial composition – and his first publication after the long silence since 1913! He was well informed as to musical trends among the young French composers, and they did not seem to shock him, on the contrary, any more than they shocked Berg, or even Webern, who particularly liked Darius's chamber symphonies and *Le Boeuf sur le Toit*!

How much of Schönberg's music did Milhaud actually know?

I think he had a very good knowledge at least of the atonal works. When he went to see Schönberg in Vienna he bought the scores of *Die glückliche Hand* and *Erwartung*, and Schönberg gave Darius his score of the Five Orchestral Pieces, marked with his own conducting annotations for the first performance.

They had great esteem for each other and Darius always kept in touch with Schönberg. During the Second World War we went to see him in Hollywood very often. There was a whole colony of Austrians in the region which had grown up around Alma Mahler and Werfel.

Did you get to know Alma Mahler very well?

Fairly well. I met her several times. She was the most beautiful woman I have ever met. Although she had been the inspiration and companion of creative artists, she had lost nothing of her own personality. In May 1940, just after the invasion of the Netherlands, we had met Alma and Werfel in Paris. They were hoping to travel to the USA but Werfel as a Czech citizen could not get a visa. It was very worrying for them. They had decided to go to Spain, but had to stay a very long time in Lourdes before they found a guide who would agree to take them secretly across the border. They really were in desperate straits. It was then that Werfel made a vow to write a book about Saint Bernadette of Lourdes if they should reach safety. Happily they did get to the USA, so Werfel wrote his book. I remember they were dining with us in Los Angeles one day when Werfel was called to the telephone. He was told that his book was to be turned into a film, and that of course guaranteed their financial security.

We had a lot of friends in the region. The atmosphere at the Schönbergs was very gay and relaxed. The Master was particularly alert and vivacious and took part in the children's games, tennis above all. He lived not far from the Stravinskys and we were always astonished that they had no contact at all. They were like African kings, each waiting for the other, but nobody came . . . Gertrude Schönberg was always anxious to find out if we had seen the Stravinskys before we called on her.

Was Stravinsky a very sociable person?

He was very Russian! – just as his music has no relationship with anything Latin; it is ritualistic. He liked to have friends round and was fond of eating and drinking – drinking especially! His friends knew that, and shortly after the war he received from one of them several bottles of Bordeaux. Igor was summoned to the customs, where he was asked for the import licence. He didn't have one of course, so the customs officer smashed all twenty-four bottles of wine right in front of him. Igor was desperate!

Do you think he was happy in the USA?

I think so. He had a few friends. As Europeans we all needed to keep in close contact because we were all in the same situation, with the same fears and hopes, and we were all deprived of our home countries. For Igor this exile had started long before, ever since he had left Russia in 1917. He was extremely worried because he had a daughter with tuberculosis in a sanatorium in France and it was materially impossible to send her any money. Darius suggested he ask his father to send some. Igor was more than grateful and it brought us closer still.

He and his wife spent two days with us at Mills College. Igor had agreed to give a lecture. Nadia Boulanger decided to come as well and suggested she play some piano duets with Igor. I attended the rehearsal. She was very severe and at one point slapped Igor's hand saying 'No, Igor, it isn't right. Count!' He always had a tendency to be a bit bent, but at that moment, I can tell you, his head was lower than his chest. It was as if no one was there! It is strange, but sometimes he was very shy – and he always had 'nerves' – stage fright. I saw that for myself when I was the reciter in *Perséphone*. We were recording in New York for the NBC. It was not difficult but there was this spot! I had asked Igor to look at me to give me my cue, but he kept his head buried in the score from start to finish. We did it together again in Turin. I had worked hard on it so I should not have to ask for help at all. Igor was much relieved. After the concert he said to me, 'Oh! How you've improved!' All the same, and independently of my admiration for him, I was very fond of Igor. He had the reputation of being something of a money eater, but why shouldn't he be paid what he was worth? For once a composer could be well paid. Bravo! Let's be happy about it. He had been extremely generous to me that time in New York as he

11. Darius with Stravinsky, 1952

thought that the NBC hadn't paid me enough, so he gave me a cheque out of his own pocket. I bought a suit with the money which I called 'Perséphone'!

I myself produced *Mavra* and *The Soldier's Tale* in Aspen and I was the reciter in a recording of the latter. It was quite a strange experience. *The Soldier's Tale* was to be in French on one side of the record and in English on the other. You can't imagine how I worked at it! The English accent of my two partners was even worse than mine – and that gave me some courage!

As your English is so good, I think we must make some allowances for modesty there! Stokowsky was the conductor for *The Soldier's Tale*, wasn't he?

Yes. At least so I was told.

What do you mean?

Well, although he was the conductor, I never saw him! You see the music was recorded independently of the recitation. Don't ask me why! As reciters we just had to imagine what would be suitable, and then Stokowsky and the musicians played to a recording of our recitation, with the consequence that the coordination was totally artificial and indeed the tempos were quite wrong at times.

Was that experience an exception in your long career as a reciter?

Fortunately, yes!

Did you have a favourite part as reciter?

Apart from Darius's works, which were of course always especially special, my favourite was undoubtedly *Perséphone*.

Perhaps we might conclude this section on Stravinsky with your impressions of his influence after World War II – or perhaps rather his lack of influence?

You are right to cast doubt on his influence after the war. The grip that serialism had on composers no doubt surprised Stravinsky. After all serialism had been 'invented' back in the early twenties. I think he did suffer because of it, and it was that perhaps that encouraged his relationship with a certain young conductor from New York. How did Robert Craft become an intimate of the Stravinsky household? Doubtless as in Russian novels, where there is always a stranger in the family! His influence became such that it was impossible to see the Stravinskys when we were in Los Angeles – and all their friends were in the same boat. It was very distressing. Nonetheless Igor managed to escape from time to time and he would come to see us for a short while. Then several years went by and we met him again in Rome in 1963 under very unusual circumstances. It was the first ecumenical concert organized by Italian radio in the presence of Pope Paul VI and various composers represented their respective religions. Malipiero was there as a

Roman Catholic, Igor as an Orthodox, Milhaud as a Jew, and a piece of Sibelius was played to represent the Protestants. It was a very moving concert. Igor seemed to us to be much changed; he had aged and was unsteady on his feet. The Director of the RAI had invited us all to dinner, and Igor fainted during the meal. Despite that, he left Rome at dawn the next day. When we said goodbye he kissed us with tenderness and emotion. Tears were in his eyes, and I shall never forget his look of anguish.

You must have met many other foreign composers in the USA during the war?

Not all that many in fact, but I must tell you about Bartók, whom we knew already. We had been to Budapest in 1928 to spend a few days with our friend Audrey Parr – her husband was the British Ambassador to Hungary. Bartók had been kind enough to invite us to his home even though his wife was very ill. His studio was very striking, with electric wires everywhere running from gramophone loudspeakers. He achieved quite prodigious work collecting songs of exceptional beauty from the furthest and most primitive reaches of Hungary. We met him several times at festivals. In such places he would be so intimidated that he would almost hang on Kodály's arm. And yet this man who seemed so timid had the courage to leave Hungary without being forced to do so, simply because he disapproved of the political situation. He arrived in the States with his young wife and led an extremely difficult existence, as his music was not performed and he didn't receive any commissions.

In 1945 Milhaud was giving a lecture in Columbia University and to his surprise he caught sight of Bartók in the audience. He looked awfully pale and weak. After the lecture he came round to see Milhaud and asked, 'Is it true that you have an incurable disease, as I have?' I don't know what Milhaud answered but he had been very struck by Bartók's appearance and indeed he died shortly afterwards – and as soon as he died, his music was performed constantly all over the place!

I've always been struck by the sheer amount of travel tha
Milhaud undertook throughout his life, not least when he had to
be in a wheelchair. Did he like to travel? Didn't it tire him?

All his life Milhaud was an enthusiastic traveller, and never go
tired of it! Despite his physical condition we sometimes travelled
under very difficult circumstances – but nothing stopped him!
cannot begin to count the number of times for example we went to
Brussels. Certainly there were reasons, as our friend Paul Collaer
had very many of Milhaud's works performed there, but also
Darius liked to spend a few days at his home in Malines and ever
to work there. Travel stimulated him.

To the point of actually composing while travelling . . .

Yes, for example working on *Les Euménides* on the boat back from
Brazil, composing part of his Fourth Symphony in the Atlantic and
Pacific Oceans, or, much later, composing a *Sonatine à Trois* or
the train between Chicago and Oakland. The first time he com
posed in a train was in 1927 between New York and Minneapolis
In those days one had to spend a lot of time simply to get from one
place to another. Nowadays you hardly have time to read the safety
instructions! Darius would even compose when we went shopping
I would dash into a shop to get a few things and he would pull out
a manuscript book and work on his current composition while he
waited for me!

When he was young, before it became too painful, he went on
long walks or horse rides. We replaced this later on with daily car
rides. In Aix after his work we would drive for miles discovering
new roads. It was a necessary escape for him, one that lasted right
up to the end of his life. We would also travel abroad by car, to
Belgium of course, but Germany as well, and Italy.

And the Soviet Union?

Ah, that would have been too much! You are referring, I presume,
to the trip we made to Moscow and Leningrad in 1926. By the way,
I must tell you that not far from where I live is a road named after

the latter city, and in the course of my life I have seen it follow all the changes in name of the city itself. First *rue Saint Pétersbourg*, then *rue de Pétrograd*, then *rue de Leningrad*, and now full circle back to *rue Saint Pétersbourg*! Despite this, Darius's *Soirées de Pétrograd* have not changed their name!

Though some Germans had previously been invited, Milhaud was the first French composer to be invited to the USSR to give some concerts. We went with Jean Wiéner. The public in Moscow and Leningrad was avid to hear contemporary French music, and in addition Jean initiated them into syncopated music, which was still unknown to them. American rhythms were a genuine revelation for them, and after the concert young musicians jumped up on stage and tried to imitate Jean.

Our trip was extremely interesting. We naturally went to the theatre, to the museum, even to the Conservatory where we visited Glazunov. I don't think our visit left much impression on him as he was completely drunk. We even visited a primary school. The pupils had the right to edit a newspaper in which they could openly express their criticisms and demands. This amazed us; it was not possible in France. Darius received the visit of a young man who seemed very intimidated. He showed Darius a symphony he had just composed, and it immediately gave Darius an inkling of what a brilliant future awaited that young man who was only eighteen. It was Shostakovich.

Of course the charming interpreter never left us for a second, which was in fact rather convenient. All the same we felt we had to be somewhat circumspect as we risked precipitating a catastrophe through inadvertence. When Jean Wiéner delivered some knitted clothing to the parents of some émigrés, he never suspected that he might have caused them to be arrested – and us also. One day we noticed a slight tear in the wallpaper of our hotel room and we suspected there was a microphone hidden there, so we got into the habit of standing in front of it every evening and saying in a very loud voice that we were so happy to be in Russia, that it must be so pleasant to live there.

We felt rather ashamed of ourselves in being able to eat properly for the Russians were already experiencing food shortages, but what could we do to help them? What was distressing was that if we asked for an egg for our breakfast, twelve eggs would arrive, and we knew they had nothing to eat. We left Russia with a certain melancholy. We had met so many charming, friendly, enthusiastic people there. Indeed our trip left a deep impression on us. It proved difficult to make our friends understand what we had come across. The embarrassment passed fortunately, but our stay in the USSR remained alive in our memories.

And after that you went to America?

Yes. Milhaud just had time to compose the *Carnaval d'Aix* in order to have a new piece to perform on tour.

Where did the tour start?

In New York. Darius played the *Carnaval* under Mengelberg's direction. We spent several days with some friends, Robert Schmitz and his wife. It was Robert who organized our tour, under the auspices of his association Pro Musica. He was an excellent pianist. He settled in New York shortly after World War I. He was a very successful teacher and organized several schools in various towns. It was then that he had the idea of bringing French composers over to present their works to American audiences. He was very friendly with Ives, whose piano music he had performed before it had been discovered and appreciated by his compatriots. Ives invited us to lunch. He was a charming, modest, humble man, and seemed unaware of his own worth.

Our first stop was Boston. Walter Damrosch had the unusual idea of calling his concert series 'Pleasant and unpleasant music', making the public decide into which category it would place the *Ballade* that Darius had just played. I cannot remember what their verdict was, though I have no doubt they decided the work was unpleasant!

We were staying in a little hotel the Schmitzes had recommended. They even told us that if we needed anything the manager would help us. Now this was during Prohibition. I liked to have a little rum with me in case of an attack of flu, and I knew that if you already had a stock of wine before Prohibition you did not have to destroy it. So one morning I asked the manager for a little rum. The waiter at once brought us some and also a bottle of fine Bordeaux. Shortly afterwards the manager called to find out if we had enjoyed the wine. He couldn't imagine that we had been able to resist drinking this rare commodity, even at 9 a.m.! I felt obliged to tell an untruth!! We had in fact decided to keep it for Christmas dinner with some friends in Alabama. And it was really appreciated, because they used to drink the most horrible mixtures. I don't know how they didn't all die! Darius was extremely careful, he usually refused to drink it. But I drank it, because somebody had to. Honour had to be saved!

The train journey was fascinating. We were struck by the similarity between the great open spaces all covered with snow and the deserted plains of Russia. But of course in other respects America was quite different. We met up with a French woman friend, Jeanne Herscher, in Birmingham. She taught music there in a conservatory and was researching into Red Indian music. Together we attended a service in a little church with a black congregation. The minister knew we were French, but he said to us, exactly as if we were American, 'Why do you give us your children to nurse, why do you let us stay in your houses, knowing you will not be robbed – why do you show confidence in us and then treat us as you do, that is, very badly?' He asked his mother to stand up; she had been a slave as a young girl. Then he began to preach, starting in a very low voice and very slowly. Gradually it got higher and higher and louder and louder, more and more exciting, and by the time half a dozen women started screaming and rolling about on the floor you wondered if it would ever stop! You had the impression anything could happen. He was an extraordinary preacher – and an extraordinary actor. Apart from that, we felt this segregation of two races everywhere: it was awkward, one was ill at ease.

Not in Europe at least, in France.

Don't be so sure! Sometime in 1930 we had learned that there was a nightclub in Paris that closed its doors to negroes so as not to upset its American clientèle. So one evening, with some friends, we invited a negro we knew to come along, and settled down at a table in a very elegant nightclub. In turn my friends and I danced with this 'undesirable', and when the manager asked us to stop we reacted in such a way that it displeased the Americans who felt obliged to leave the place. We were victims of the same ostracism – the other way round – in New Orleans. We were refused entry to see an operetta in a small theatre and when we demanded to speak to the manager he suggested, as we were French, that we see the show from his own office: there was a little window with a view onto the stage.

We continued our tour for several weeks, visiting different cities very rapidly. We were greatly looking forward to having a quiet stay in Los Angeles, without the constant attendance of the charming ladies of Pro Musica, who very generously put themselves at our disposal, without leaving us a moment of independence.

We had been in L.A. a short while and were preparing for a walk to the Pacific Ocean, when the President of Pro Musica suddenly arrived. 'What can I do for you?', she said. 'Absolutely nothing, thank you', we replied, 'we shall see you tomorrow. Good-bye!'. But when we said we wanted to go for a walk to see the Pacific Ocean, she looked at us with stupefaction and told us in authoritative tones, 'I'm going to drive you there then.' And she did! She drove for hours, as the distances in L.A. are such as to be quite unimaginable. When we arrived at Santa Monica, she turned to us and said, 'That's it! That's the Pacific!' The ocean was a dark, almost invisible mass as there was a slight mist, and the daylight was already fading!

What else did you do in Los Angeles?

Of course, we visited the Hollywood studios. We met some very friendly actors including Mary Pickford and Douglas Fairbanks who invited us to tea. They were absolutely charming and relaxed. Mary Pickford had the typical reaction of most small women when she asked me to take my shoes off in order to find out which of us was the taller. We were exactly the same size. Honour was saved!

Was Milhaud ever asked to write a score for a Hollywood film?

Once, in 1946, for a production by Albert Lewin: *The Private Affairs of Bel-Ami*, based on a novel by Guy de Maupassant. Yet he was not popular in the studio. A composer who orchestrates his own music and decides to conduct the recording was unheard of! He knew he would never be asked again.

I believe René Clair and Jean Renoir were in Los Angeles at that time. Was there ever any question of collaboration with Milhaud?

None of them ever proposed a collaboration, though we did see Jean Renoir several times during our later stay in America. He organized a film festival in San Francisco and asked Milhaud to be on the jury. He came to lunch once with a group of French actors: Jean Marais, Gérard Philippe, Micheline Presle, Françoise Arnoul. After lunch they all got around the piano to sing together. The only piece of music they knew was the folksong 'Alouette, gentille alouette'!

Did Milhaud give a concert in San Francisco then?

No. We went there because I very much wanted to see the place where my maternal grandfather had spent all his life. For me, who never knew him, he was like someone in a legend.

I remember we arrived in San Francisco fairly late in the evening. The station is on the other side of the bay, and as in those days there was no bridge across it, we reached the city by boat. Crossing the bay in the night was magical. Little did we know that the city would become so familiar to us fifteen years later – without losing any of its magic!

The end of our stay was approaching so we booked our passage on an English cargo-ship. During the crossing Darius asked me to fetch a book from the ship's library, in French preferably. There was only one, the memoirs of a journey made by an officer of Maximilian's court in Mexico. Darius knew nothing about the Emperor Maximilian, though of course he had seen Manet's famous painting of his execution. The book fascinated him.

Maximilian was a Habsburg and had married the King of Belgium's daughter Carlotta, a very ambitious woman. The Habsburg family wanted to set up a monarch in Mexico to stand up against the revolutionaries. Napoleon III backed the project, and so Maximilian became Emperor of Mexico. However, he was a dreamy character, with a liberal disposition, weak and, above all, human. He did not have the power to fight the Mexicans and, as he failed, was abandoned by everyone. Carlotta went to Europe to try to raise help in order to save her husband. The author of the memoirs that had so fascinated Darius had accompanied the Empress on this final, fruitless journey.

Darius was overwhelmed by what he had read, and it is a curious thing, but he was literally pursued by this figure. We had only just arrived in Paris when we bought the memoirs of Count Corti, which had just been published. He had been ambassador at the time of Maximilian. We had to go to Brussels for a concert before going to see Emil Hertzka, the director of Universal Edition, who had invited us to Vienna. The Belgian papers were full of pictures and stories about Maximilian and Carlotta, his unfortunate wife who had just died. She was the king's aunt and had lived near Brussels as something of a recluse as she had been mentally unstable for some years. Darius naturally carried on reading the Corti memoirs during his visit to Hertzka. He even confided in the publisher that he would like to write a historical opera based on Maximilian. Hertzka then told him that Franz Werfel had written a play on the subject which was having a great success in Germany.

Darius had met Werfel in 1922 at Alma Mahler's and he at once got in touch with him. When he did so it was to learn that the writer had just received a French translation of his play *Juarez and Maximilian*! Juarez had been the leader of the revolutionaries opposed to Maximilian. Even though he is never seen in the play, he is really the active element in the whole story and his influence is constantly felt.

After the meeting everything went very quickly. Werfel agreed to the preparation of a libretto from his play, Armand Lunel was to make a French adaptation of the German text, Hertzka was to publish the work, and Milhaud was about to start composing when he received a letter from Claudel asking him to see him as soon as possible.

We went by car to Claudel's house at Brangues, in southern France. Claudel had retired to his study with Darius to read him the first part of *Christophe Colomb*. Darius was instantly attracted by the variety of scenes, by the figure of Columbus and, in short, without bothering about projects that were already in hand, set to work to compose the opera *Christophe Colomb*. It was only two years later, after the first performance of *Colomb* in Berlin, that he started to compose *Maximilien* . . .

Why was *Christophe Colomb* not first performed in Paris?

Because the chorus of the Opera was not good enough at that time. The chorus has an almost continuous role in the action of the opera, which makes things very difficult. That is why Claudel suggested that the chorus should stand without moving, holding the score in front of themselves, as in a church or temple, and that was how it was done in Berlin.

Could you describe the style of the production?

Claudel's conception included several new theatrical ideas. The main action takes place when Columbus is very old, though several scenes show him aged thirty years younger. The flashback had never been used in opera before. There were also present on stage two different versions of Columbus himself: the historical one and the Columbus of posterity, the one found in history books and immortalized in statues. And for the first time in an opera, one could see moving film showing scenes a little different from what was happening simultaneously on stage.

Claudel's view of Columbus is of a man who brings Christianity to the new world (whether for better or for worse is another matter!) and who is inspired by two things: a passion for adventure, nurtured by reading about Marco Polo when he was young (is there another world?), and something which is indicative of Claudel's mysticism. Queen Isabella of Spain is given a dove as a child. She puts her ring on the dove's foot and the dove flies into Columbus's room. Columbus takes the ring and so everything that is done is done in the Queen's name. There is a mystical marriage between Columbus's mind – his poetical, human, honourable side – and Isabella, to whom he eventually gives the kingdom he has discovered. At the end of the opera she cannot reach the kingdom of Heaven without Columbus. This mystical element is constantly at work in the action of the opera.

What was the Berlin performance like?

Absolutely marvellous! Erich Kleiber was a great conductor and worked very hard. The opera was a considerable success and was even revived the following year, although the National Socialist movement was already making itself felt very strongly.

Was it ever performed in France?

It was performed in a concert version several times – the first time conducted by Pierre Monteux with a choir from the provinces – but it was not staged in France until 1985, in Marseilles.

What is its relationship to Milhaud's later *Christophe Colomb*?

You mean the incidental music Darius wrote in 1952? Jean-Louis Barrault had already staged several Claudel plays and was going to put on *Le Livre de Christophe Colomb*, to give the play its full title. Claudel asked Darius to write the music.

It was rather painful for Milhaud to return to such a subject. When writing an opera he was free to write as he wished – what the critics or the public might think was frankly of no consideration. But for incidental music he had to please the public or at any rate take into account the effect his music would have on it. The music was necessarily functional. However, he did it out of friendship for Claudel. There is nothing in common between the two works (except for one theme from the opera which Claudel asked Milhaud to reuse), though the text is just the same. That said, there is one identical feature to both works. The first act is very factual, unfolding the basic story of Columbus's expedition. The second act is more abstract: Columbus has no money left, just debts, and comes back to Spain in despair; even his mule is taken away from him, the only friend he had left. The opera ends with the death of Isabella, who calls for her friend Columbus to come to her. But the second act never had the same success as the first. Audiences were taken aback by its stricter, more austere presentation. After the first performance in Berlin, Darius had already felt it necessary to make some cuts in this part. So stupidly, as a joke, when we were coming back from the Théâtre Marigny where Barrault had staged a remarkable performance of *Christophe Colomb*, I said to Darius, 'Why don't you put the acts the other way round?' 'Oh!' said Darius, 'it's perfect!'. I forgot all about it, but the following day he called Claudel who told him 'I gave you my play; do with it what you want! And if necessary I shall write a little text to tie up with the inversion of the acts' – and he did so! Now when Darius had an idea, he was as stubborn as could be – he would never go back on it or waste time thinking it over, although he would meditate a long time before actually writing the notes of a score. I was terrified about the change in *Colomb*, and the publisher was not in favour of it either. As I had been responsible for the suggestion I insisted that Milhaud think hard about it before working on it, not that there are any real musical changes. But there was nothing to be done: it was settled!

What is the situation now with this work?

You can choose either the first or the second version. The first version was performed in Marseilles, the second in Compiègne in 1992. If means are modest, it is possible to stage only the part which ends with the arrival in America. Otherwise there is always the play with the incidental music. Madame Claudel always used to refer to *Christophe Colomb* as 'yours' when she meant the opera and 'ours' when she meant the play.

What happened to *Maximilien* then?

After the success of *Christophe Colomb* in Berlin, questions were raised in parliament. Several members were astonished that a work by Claudel and Milhaud should receive its first performance

12. *Maximilien*, Paris Opera, 1932: décor by Raoul Dufy

abroad. It was this that decided the director of the Paris Opera, Jacques Rouché, to stage *Maximilien*.

What part does the chorus play in this work?

The chorus part is quite normal, without any particular difficulties. The drama is mainly expressed by duos and airs 'alla Verdi'. It is a very lyrical and dramatic work. I wouldn't say there is a Verdi influence on Milhaud's music, but there is a shared tradition, not concretely felt, more a question of a spiritual relationship, a matter of understanding. Darius felt that he and Verdi belonged to the same race, the same species.

What pushed Milhaud to write historical operas? – there's *Bolivar* as well . . .

That's true! And even *David*. I think there are several reasons. For the heroes of all these operas, morality, religion and justice come together in a drama of conscience. Maximilian understood the right of the Mexican people to rise up against European domination. Bolivar fought to free the people from Spanish domination. Bolivar and Columbus were idolized, honoured, fêted, until things changed and they were abandoned by everyone. It was precisely this human drama that was part of the attraction for Darius.

Those were the big, epic operas. But Milhaud was also very successful with chamber opera . . .

The first was *Les Malheurs d'Orphée*. Darius had long wanted to write an 'Orpheus', recounting the story of a man who finds his beloved only in death. Naturally he turned to his friend Lunel for the libretto.

They decided to transpose the Greek legend, setting it in the Camargue where they used to go a lot in their younger days. They had often attended the festivities in late May celebrating the three Saint Marys and their black servant Sarah who had landed there. Sarah was the patron saint of the gypsies. In the opera Orpheus

13. *From left to right:* Armand Lunel, Milhaud, Jean Hugo, at L'Enclos, 1923

became a healer, looking after the animals as well as the inhabitants of his village. He gets on well with his neighbours, and falls in love with a gypsy girl, Eurydice, whom he saw dancing during a pilgrimage to Saintes-Maries-de-la-Mer. Of course, in the mind of the gypsies a union of this sort was impossible, and Eurydice runs away, knowing that if her family catch her she will be killed, together with her lover.

Following his neighbours' advice, Orpheus flees into the mountains with Eurydice. But Eurydice is mortally afflicted with a mysterious illness. She dies, and Orpheus, desperate, is left alone, surrounded by the animals he takes care of. The transposition of the myth continues: Eurydice's three sisters, who believe that he killed her, arrive like the legendary Bacchantes and kill him. But Orpheus dies happy, for he will soon be with his beloved.

The composition of *Les Malheurs d'Orphée* was hardly over when Lunel proposed another subject to Darius. The ancestors of Lunel and of Milhaud had lived in Carpentras since the thirteenth century. The Comtat Venaissin was then under the control of the Pope. The Jews were well treated, much better than in the kingdom of France. Despite having to pay all sorts of taxes, they felt they were in a privileged position. Once a year they asked the Cardinal Bishop permission to present the traditional play of *Esther* outside the ghetto in the town square. Lunel based his play *Esther de Carpentras* on anecdotes that his grandfather had told him, and on an eighteenth-century play. He imagines that the Bishop – who is very young and has just arrived in Carpentras from Rome – grants the Jews their request. So the play, *Esther*, takes place. It proceeds quite normally until suddenly the Bishop appears, climbs up on stage and takes the place of the actor playing Assuérus. He orders his Minister to read an edict threatening the Jews with death or exile if they refuse to convert. Unaware of the substitution, the actress playing Esther sings a moving expression of her faith, declaring that she and her fellow-believers would face death rather than give up their beliefs. Moved by Esther's sincerity – and perhaps by her beauty – the Bishop renounces his project of expulsion. Surrounded by the choristers singing a canticle, the Bishop goes back to his residence. The Jews join in with a hymn of thanksgiving.

Lunel's libretto gave Milhaud the opportunity of composing a whole host of different airs for different characters. It is an extremely lively work in which carefree gaiety follows upon drama, but the whole work is dominated by a deep religious feeling.

What about Milhaud's other opera of that time, *Le Pauvre Matelot*?

That was in fact his second chamber opera. It has a libretto by Jean Cocteau, written in fact for Georges Auric, but he was too busy to use it. Darius was delighted to take it over.

The story runs like this: in a little street in a port there are two cafés, one belonging to a sailor's wife, one to his friend – nobody has a name in this opera. The sailor had left for sea fifteen years before and has never been heard of since. His wife has remained faithful to him, feeling sure he will come back one day.

And he does come back, but is afraid of not being recognized, so he first goes to see his friend, who informs him that his wife has been faithful but that she has a lot of financial problems. The next evening the sailor goes to see his wife, pretending to be a friend of her husband who had charged him to bring her news and tell her he would be coming home soon, though not rich – in fact covered with debts. He boasts that he had more luck than him, showing her the pearls he has in his pocket. He then asks if he could be put up for the night. 'You have brought me news of my husband,' she says. 'Make yourself at home.' The sailor beds down for the night, and while he is sleeping the wife kills him with a hammer, then takes the pearls 'in order to save my husband'. The curtain falls before she realizes her mistake.

At the time of the first performance of *Le Pauvre Matelot* the orchestral musicians still had the right to send a substitute for a concert if they had some other engagement – making a recording for example. The result was that, for the première, seventeen musicians sight-read the score of *Le Pauvre Matelot*! A week later it was put on at the Monnaie in Brussels. Georges Auric, who had attended the Paris performances, came to the Monnaie and asked Milhaud if he had reorchestrated his score, as it sounded completely different!

Several years later Darius made a version for chamber orchestra at the request of Hermann Scherchen who wanted to take it on tour, and it's always been played like that since. *Le Pauvre Matelot* and *Les Malheurs d'Orphée* are Milhaud's most popular operas and were played very frequently in Germany before the war. As far as *Esther de Carpentras* is concerned, it often comes as a surprise to realize that it was in fact written for quite a large orchestra, and I thought that nowadays an *opéra-bouffe* would be difficult to stage in such conditions. So, after asking the advice of several musician friends, I took the decision to have a reduced orchestration made. It was in this version for chamber orchestra that *Esther* was recently staged in New York and Carpentras.

Milhaud's remaining chamber opera is *Fiesta*, the subject of which is not unrelated to that of *Le Pauvre Matelot*: the absurd and fatality are the dominant elements. The libretto is by Boris Vian, who was inspired by a real incident. He had been in a café along the Saint Martin Canal in Paris one winter's day. A cat had nearly drowned in the canal and had been brought into the café. It was wrapped in towels and given milk. When the cat revived it started to bite and scratch everyone – so it was thrown back into the canal.

Fiesta takes place on an island in the Pacific. Nothing ever happens there, except that from time to time, miraculously, a boat is wrecked and the survivors are brought ashore. It is an opportunity for the islanders to improvise a quick fiesta. On this occasion everyone crowds round the shipwrecked sailor and tries to bring him back to life. A young woman manages to do this, but when the sailor regains consciousness he shows not the slightest gratitude. His only interest is in the young woman herself, and her lover quickly becomes jealous, eventually stabbing the sailor to death. Everyone leaves the stage, except for three old men who start to sing a ballad about a man who was washed up by the sea, who fell in love with a girl, who got a knife in his back, so the poor man died, so back to the sea he had to go – and the old men throw his body back into the water.

Where was *Fiesta* staged?

Milhaud wrote it in 1958 at Scherchen's request for the Berlin Festival. He was a good friend; we had known him since 1929 when he conducted *Le Retour de l'Enfant Prodigue* in Baden Baden.

14. Directing *Fiesta*, Mills College, 1965

Milhaud went there several times, I think?

Yes. Paul Hindemith directed the festival and invited Milhaud on several occasions. Hindemith wanted new musical experiences to be featured every year: music for amateurs, for film, cantatas . . . In 1927 he had the idea of staging very short lyric works. Darius was very proud because his contribution, *L'Enlèvement d'Europe*, was the shortest, lasting barely ten minutes! His publisher, Emil Hertzka, said they were unable to publish such a short work: Milhaud would have to write a trilogy. The author of the libretto, Henri Hoppenot, set to work again and so there are three 'minute-operas' lasting twenty-eight minutes in all. For all their brevity, they are genuine mythological dramas.

It was also for Baden Baden that Darius composed his first film score, for Cavalcanti's *La P'tite Lilie*. The recording was to take place in Berlin. The director Hans Richter was finishing the editing

of his film *Vormittagsspuck* which was to be shown at the same
time as *La P'tite Lilie*. Milhaud agreed to make a brief appearance
in the film.

In Baden Baden, Hindemith was taken up day and night finishing
his score for *Vormittagsspuck*, and he had to transcribe the score
onto a special device. Hindemith suggested Darius might like to try
out this new cinematographic apparatus which enabled one to project the image on the film at the same time as work on the sound
track. Darius liked the idea, got hold of the newsreel items for the
week and so wrote music for 'Aviators' Official Reception'
'Kangaroo Boxer', 'The Derby', etc. The pieces are very much in the
style of his chamber symphonies.

Are they concert pieces?

Absolutely – they form a suite called *Actualités*.

**It is very rare for a film score to be suitable for concert perfor-
mance, and Milhaud wrote quite a lot of film music. Did he try to
rescue such music when he could?**

On occasion, yes. For instance, he wrote the music for André
Malraux's film *L'Espoir*, made after the Spanish Civil War. In it
there is a particularly striking scene when the peasants bring back
into the valley the body of a Republican aviator who had been
killed or wounded as he bombed the bridge of Teruel. A very long
procession winds its way in front of the whole population of the
region, lined up along the route. It creates a moving atmosphere
and this gave Milhaud the opportunity of writing a ten-minute
Cortège Funèbre which can be played independently of the film. He
conducted the first concert performance in New York in July 1940
in memory of the war dead.

There is also the wind quintet *Divertissement*, from his music to
Gauguin, a film by Alain Resnais; *La Cheminée du Roi René*, from
Cavalcade d'Amour, *L'Album de Madame Bovary* (and some
songs and piano waltzes) from Renoir's film. That said, it's not
much from twenty or so scores!

Why did Milhaud write so many?

It was not easy to earn your living as a composer before the war. Nowadays it's a lot easier to get a teaching job, for example.

Was the same true for incidental music, of which Milhaud also wrote a considerable quantity?

The problem is very much the same. It is exceptional when music can be extracted successfully from a particular dramatic context and used in a concert. It does sometimes happen. There is however a difference in that the relationship between composer and stage producer can be much more personal than is the case with the cinema. If a producer is sensitive to music there can be a genuine collaboration between them, but in some cases the composer is merely treated like the decorator or the stage-carpenter. In both cases – film and incidental music – the composer has to conform with docility and patience to the demands and even caprices of the director, and has to be ready to cut out or add bars here and there. Milhaud certainly accepted this discipline with patience and humility. I well remember one evening at home when the stage producer, Jean-Louis Barrault, was pacing nervously up and down in the living room telling Darius the precise durations for the musical interventions for Giraudoux's play *Judith*. Darius very conscientiously noted them all, and in composing the score scrupulously respected the producer's wishes. The music was then recorded and when we attended the rehearsal Darius discovered that three-quarters of his score had been completely dropped!

I have already told you about his second score for *Christophe Colomb*; well, the same thing happened in reverse as it were in the case of Supervielle's play *Bolivar*. Darius wrote incidental music for it in the normal way for a performance at the Comédie Française in 1936; it required a great deal of music. In 1942 he was very keen to write an opera and at the same time his thoughts were fixed on the liberation of Europe. Both thoughts came together and Bolívar seemed the perfect subject, and he wrote the opera the following year.

What was Milhaud's first experience of incidental music?

It was with Claudel – naturally enough! In 1912 Claudel was translating Aeschylus's Oresteian trilogy and asked Darius – at almost their first meeting – to write some music for a particular point in the first play, the point at which Clytemnestra, having just killed Agamemnon, is confronted by a chorus of old men. Darius wrote music for this one scene, and went on to write more extensive incidental music for the second play in the trilogy, *Les Choéphores*. This is a much more substantial work and can be performed without the spoken scenes. It was Darius himself who decided to make a fully fledged opera of the third part, *Les Euménides*. This really is a huge work, and was not staged until 1963 by the Berlin State Opera.

However, the music for *Agamemnon* and *Les Choéphores* is not true incidental music, which is no doubt why Darius himself referred to it as simply 'music for the theatre'. His first real score of the kind was for Claudel's *Protée* in 1913. Claudel had told Darius he was 'too serious' to write the music for this comic play, but he did it nonetheless, writing for a very large orchestra – such things were possible in those days! It was also the first play in which Claudel thought of using cinema, to portray the various transformations of Proteus, although it was not until 1930 in *Christophe Colomb* that such techniques were actually realized. In 1955, for a new production, Darius wrote another score for the play, for only four instruments. In fact there were nearly always several versions of Claudel's plays, each with its own score. All very confusing for the musicologist!

One thing I've noticed in a number of Milhaud's scores of incidental music is the use of the ondes Martenot. Milhaud must have been something of a pioneer in this?

I think so! You see, incidental music sometimes allows a composer to make certain experiments and try out new sound effects. Take for example *Le Château des Papes* by André de Richaud, staged in 1932. Darius had loudspeakers installed around the theatre ceiling, and in the plague scene, which he had scored for trumpet and ondes Martenot, the public was absolutely terrified by the sound of the new instrument! As a footnote I would add that it is interesting Milhaud only ever used the ondes Martenot in incidental music, not concert works.

Did Milhaud prefer writing for any particular kind of play?

No, he wrote for all sorts; plays by contemporary writers and also classical plays: Aristophanes, Molière, and several Shakespeares – *A Winter's Tale*, *Romeo and Juliet*, *Julius Caesar*, and a *Macbeth* at the Old Vic which greatly impressed him.

Did he often go to London?

He conducted very often for the BBC, and it's amusing to think that his first contact with jazz was made in London, in 1920. The Billy Arnold Band had just come over from America and was playing in Hammersmith. Darius was thunderstruck by the new rhythms and tone-colours, to the point of thinking of writing a chamber music work directly inspired by this music.

***La Création du Monde*!**

Not yet! Wait a minute! In 1922 he left for America. During his stay in New York he spent every evening in Harlem listening to the groups from New Orleans. It was there that he discovered the jazz music that expresses the sorrow of a people complaining of the injustice of which they were victims. When he came back to France Darius brought back dozens of jazz records which he listened to night and day. More than ever he was determined to transpose the jazz idiom into a classical work. It was the director of the Ballets Suédois, Rolf de Maré, who provided the opportunity when he proposed a collaboration with Blaise Cendrars, who had just published a collection of African tales. He used one of them as the basis for 'The Creation of the World', a subject that was taken up with enthusiasm by Darius and by Léger. I remember Fernand and Blaise and Milhaud, wearing raincoats with their collars up like gangsters and with their hats on the sides of their heads, going to those little dance halls where the Martiniquais are, near the Bastille – dangerous little places. That is how *La Création du Monde* was made. Léger based his costumes on primitive Negro art. They were all extremely impressive. It was a superb spectacle! I have rarely seen such beautiful décors and costumes as those of Léger for this production. It had a tremendous success, although the critics considered it music for nightclubs, at least for a year. After that they came to regard it as classical music . . .

Did you keep up friendly relations with Léger?

Fernand was a faithful and devoted friend. We met up with him again in America during the war. He taught at Mills College for a few weeks in 1941. He was even kind enough to help me with the décors for a play of Labiche I was producing with the students.

Later, when Milhaud wrote the music for his opera *Bolivar*, he at once spoke to Léger who was in New York at the time. Fernand hoped that the New York Met would stage it. He even looked for sponsors as he had lots of contacts in New York, but his efforts were unsuccessful. It was the Paris Opera that finally staged *Bolivar* in 1950.

Did Milhaud collaborate with any other painters?

Milhaud never really collaborated with a painter to the extent of mixing in with the artist's conceptions – he was too independently minded to wish to influence the artist, or the stage producer for that matter, and respected the autonomy of others, but he did work with Braque, Derain and Masson, as well as Léger.

And Picasso?

Milhaud never had the occasion of working with him. We knew him, without having especially close ties. I was very touched to receive a superb rose-tree from him when Daniel was born, and since Daniel became an artist, this was clearly a gift from a fairy godmother!

After the war, I remember, we were driving from Menton to Aix when we passed by Vallauris, where Picasso had his studio, and decided to stop there for a moment. Picasso was kind enough to

15. Preparing for the Bastille Day dance at Mills College, 1945

bring some of his vases to the car, so that Darius could see them
without having to get the wheelchair out.

What sort of a man was he?

I knew him too little to be able to describe him in that way, but
the deep, piercing look in his eyes was unforgettable. He seemed to
absorb everything that surrounded him – on earth and even beyond.

But didn't he paint the décors for _Le Train Bleu_?

No. They were the work of the sculptor Laurens. But as Diaghilev had been struck by a painting of Picasso's representing two women running along a beach, he asked him if he could have it enlarged as the curtain for his ballet.

And the curious title?

It refers to the luxury train tourists used to take in winter to go to the Côte d'Azur. Cocteau's idea was to present a kind of danced operetta, so this necessitated light, carefree, spontaneous music alla Chabrier, and it greatly amused Darius to write the score – in two weeks flat!

Immediately after composing the ballet *Salade* – also in two weeks

16. *La Création du Monde*, 1925: décor by Fernand Léger

flat! And it was alla Schubert–Liszt that Milhaud composed a ballet for Ida Rubinstein?

Yes, *La Bien Aimée*. The subject was quite straightforward. A young girl is in love with – and loved by – a virtuoso pianist who charms her with his talent. Schubert's waltzes had already been transcribed by Liszt who piled difficulty upon difficulty. Milhaud, who by the way had never had a piano lesson in his life, though he managed to play the instrument quite respectably, made the transcriptions even more difficult by transcribing them for Pleyela. It was the first time a mechanical piano had been introduced into the orchestra.

That can't have made life easy for the conductor, Ansermet.

You're right! He was an excellent conductor, but had an unfortunate habit, about which several eminent composers had already complained, of sometimes reorchestrating a work. When Milhaud noticed that there had been a few changes in his orchestration he complained about it. Ansermet was furious and the very next day Milhaud received a letter from him which greatly amused him and which he showed to all his friends.

Do you know what Ansermet wrote in the letter?

Amongst other things, 'I am not one of those who confuse cheek with art'! Happily, quarrels do not last long between musicians, but it goes to show there are some conductors who do not accept justified criticism.

Milhaud wrote one other work for Ida Rubinstein.

Yes. Several years went by before we saw her again at Marguerite Long's. Milhaud described to her a spectacle staged by a Palestinian group that had so impressed him that we decided to go back and see it again that very evening. Ida Rubinstein asked if she could accompany us. We were somewhat embarrassed at taking this 'grand lady' to a small local theatre. The Ohel Players were performing scenes from the Old Testament in a remarkably individual manner. Ida shared our enthusiasm and at once asked Milhaud if he would agree to write a biblical work for her. Milhaud suggested he talk to Claudel about it, and in this way 'The Parable of the Wedding Feast' was born. When the score was finished, Rubinstein several times showed her admiration for it and her interest in the future spectacle . . . then she disappeared from view for several weeks. Claudel received an enthusiastic telegram . . . then she disappeared again. To cut a long story short, she never staged *La Sagesse*, as the composition is called, and never even gave a reason.

Can you imagine why she never staged it?

The main character was perhaps too austere and did not highlight her qualities enough. The chorus has an important role, and in fact the work is perhaps more oratorio than ballet.

Has it ever been danced?

Yes! At the Rome Opera in 1950, though we were in California at the time. Darius had had the opportunity of hearing his score when Manuel Rosenthal conducted it for French radio just after the war. It was very moving as Milhaud's music had, of course, been banned during the war and it was the first time his music had been played since then. Rosenthal received the score thanks to Ida Rubinstein who quite spontaneously sent it to him.

Did this experience with Rubinstein discourage Milhaud from writing other ballets?

It was certainly not the genre that attracted Milhaud the most. I have much more often heard him express the desire to write an opera, never a ballet. Yet if one proposed an interesting subject he undertook it with pleasure – and he did compose quite a lot of ballets. Some of his ballets have very serious, even mystical subjects, *Moses (The Man from Midian)* for example, written for the Ballet Theatre of New York in 1940. Rehearsals had started when they were interrupted on account of financial complications. This did not prevent Milhaud from conducting his score on New York radio under the title *Opus Americanum no 2*.

Opus Americanum no 1 was his First Symphony, I suppose?

In fact no; it was his Tenth String Quartet which he wrote on the ship sailing to America. His First Symphony was composed in Aix, in response to a commission from the Chicago Symphony Orchestra, just a few weeks before the outbreak of war.

Why did Milhaud not write symphonies before – large-scale ones, I mean, not chamber symphonies, of course, like the ones he did compose fairly early on?

For Darius writing a symphony was a task needing maturity. He did not feel himself ready before he was fifty. After that he never stopped! He wrote twelve symphonies in all, of which eight were written in the States. Even after that he continued to write symphonic works in the form of *Musique pour* . . . However, it was the Chicago commission that gave Milhaud the courage to get back to work after the declaration of war. He couldn't get over his despair at the thought of another conflict. He was unable to react to events for quite a long time. When his symphony was finished, he received a letter from the manager of the Chicago Symphony asking him to conduct his work. He answered that he did not feel like leaving his country as long as the war was on.

Then, in June 1940, the Germans entered Paris! We knew how the Jews were dealt with by them! We knew also that Milhaud was among the first on the list of intellectuals to be arrested because he was well known in Germany as a Jewish composer, and also because he did not share their right-wing ideals. I realized that if our personal situation became dangerous, Milhaud would be in trouble because he could not walk, much less run, to hide himself. Offering oneself as a sacrifice was not very sensible. I distinctly remember saying to him, 'I can do a lot of things for you, but I cannot carry you on my shoulders and hide you.' So we decided to leave.

Darius had kept the invitation from Chicago and showed it to the American consul when he applied for our three visas. The consul was not supposed to give a visa without checking with Washington, and had a perfect right not to do so. But he took the responsibility upon himself, and in fact saved not just us, but many other French men and women as well during the war.

We bought tickets for a flight from Lisbon to New York and I drove the three of us to the French–Spanish border, as there was no way of reaching Lisbon directly. The Finance Minister had asked all French citizens not to take capital out of the country. We were stupid enough to obey, so we left home with an absolute minimum. In Spain we discovered we were not allowed to take out any money that we possessed. So we bought three tickets on the sleeper for Lisbon as we did not want to leave a single peseta for Franco's Spaniards.

We settled ourselves in a very modest hotel in Lisbon, where we met an English journalist and his wife. I felt ashamed in front of the English, whom we had abandoned whilst they were continuing to fight on alone. With Philip Carr, this feeling was soon dissipated; we were all very unhappy. We spent a long time together and it was very late when we separated. In order to support a sleepless night rather better Philip lent me a copy of Shakespeare's Sonnets and I lent him my Ronsard. The next day we found out from the travel agency that the tickets we had bought in Marseilles were invalid because the value of the French franc had fallen so much. We were practically penniless, but the Ministry of Culture organized some concerts for us and lectures to give us some means of existence. Milhaud wrote to all his friends in the USA to announce our arrival and our desire to find work.

We lost hope as the days went by. It was then that we met a close friend who was travelling with the Baroness G. R. They were installed in a palace at Estoril awaiting the ship for America. One morning the Baroness asked Milhaud to accompany her to the bank. She wanted to send some money to her gardener in Toulouse so he could plant vines! Permission was refused. She was very disappointed – aghast even. Darius suggested having some money sent to the gardener by his father and for her to give us the equivalent so we could leave Lisbon.

This was how, a few days later, we were able to embark on an American freighter. On the quayside waiting with us were Jules Romains, Julien Green and Julien Duvivier. Just as we were getting on the ship a telegram was handed to Darius: it was the offer of a teaching job at Mills College. We were saved.

When Pierre Monteux had received Milhaud's letter announcing his departure for the States he had got in touch with the President of Mills College. The professor of composition had just died and the President wanted to appoint a European. Monteux spoke about Milhaud, and the miracle came about!

Of course Darius had no scores with him, apart from the manuscript of his Tenth Quartet which he had written during the transatlantic voyage. The money that Milhaud had made on his last American tour had been left in a bank over there, but again following the request of the Finance Minister, we had asked the bank to transfer it to France. We did not know whether this had been done or not. Kurt Weill was waiting for us when we arrived and he at once accompanied us to the bank. We learned that the political situation meant the money had been frozen, but we did have the right to take out a small sum.

With this money we bought a second-hand car, which cost the same as three rail tickets to Mills! So we drove there – I ought to say, I drove there.

All the way across America!

And it was a long way – superb and monotonous! One drives for miles and miles without seeing a house, nothing except cars coming in the other direction. We tried in vain to make out the spire of a church or the roof of a building. After ten days' travelling, we arrived in California. We were temporarily housed with our friend Robert Schmitz and his wife. They lived right near the college, as their daughter studied there. We got to know the ups and downs of being tenants: only able to stay in a house for a couple of months because the owner decided to come back before the end of his sabbatical; the violence of a cantankerous owner who throws you out because you have a dog . . . Our third home was too far from the college, but otherwise was pleasant and the owner charming. Then we had a bungalow in which the rooms were so small I had to leave the bedroom so Darius could get up!

Finally the President of Mills decided to have a house built for

Milhaud in the college garden. I tried to dissuade her; I was convinced that the war would soon be over and we should then leave for France. Wishful thinking, alas!

We went to San Francisco very often to see our friends the Monteux. They were kind enough to invite us to all his concerts, something that delighted us. In those days it was the custom to programme one or two contemporary works in each concert. A few months after our arrival we learned that some cousins of ours had settled a few miles away in Berkeley. So you can see how privileged we were and that, although so far from France, we were not isolated.

What about the teaching?

Milhaud adapted himself quite remarkably to his new role as a teacher. He managed to organize his daily life so that he always had the time to compose and even have some leisure. His colleagues quickly realized they could ask his advice if necessary, but he was not 'faculty minded', and it was best to spare him administrative chores.

Was teaching in Mills much different from teaching in France?

Quite different. In France the students studied only music. In Mills on the other hand Darius was delighted to notice that although most of his students had no intention of following a musical career, music was a part of the curriculum and consequently of their general culture, and he was able to teach them as if they were future professional musicians. He never had to adapt himself to an inferior level of teaching, and was quite surprised at the serious approach of many of the students for whom music was not the main subject. Some of them could as well have taken tennis, cookery or history as a major. Of course some did continue composing during the summer vacation. The classes were mixed. The American government gave their soldiers bursaries enabling them to continue studies interrupted by the war. This was how Darius came to have several students he referred to as his 'Mills Boys'. The name was particularly suitable as they were all excellent jazz musicians who earned their living playing in the San Francisco bars. The most famous of the lot is Dave Brubeck.

Milhaud's prime concern was always to understand the path most suitable for a particular student. He advised them to acquire solid technique so they could apply themselves to composition with independence and could develop their own personality. He never discouraged anyone. For example, Dave's brother was an assistant in the music department at Mills and a composer, his mother was the head of music somewhere and he had another brother who was a teacher. So the boy felt a little confused because his talents didn't lie at all in that direction. One day Darius asked him 'What do you really enjoy doing?' and he said 'Playing boogie-woogie.' 'So why are you trying to do something else? Learn your technique, because through technique you will be free. That's the path you have to follow.' It saved him, and later on, in recognition, Dave named his elder son Darius.

What was it like being two French people over there?

We felt very clearly that the USA was a neutral country. Without wanting to upset anyone, we wanted to do what we could for our own. As far as Milhaud was concerned, his presence at Mills was prestigious enough to represent France. The other universities in the region were envious of Mills for this reason.

We were a united French family, but quite informal. We would have 'open house' and offered good things to eat that were out of the ordinary. Until Pearl Harbor, the Californians were unaware of the war, unlike the New Yorkers: there, passers-by had bombarded us with questions as soon as we arrived from Europe, asking us, in French even, what had happened to France. California looked to other continents, and of course they were at peace at that time.

And what about you?

I did everything in my power to make myself friendly and popular so as to interest as many people as possible in the fate of Europe. As far as teaching was concerned, this was easy. I intoxicated my students by making them learn French drama and making them act out French plays. I also agreed to give lectures in schools. One of them was called 'Impressions of a Foreign Mother'! It was fascinating!

What is more, as the College was quite close to San Francisco, the French consuls, even though they worked for the Vichy government, would send along French visitors who were staying for an indefinite period in San Francisco waiting for a connection to Nouméa, a French possession out in the Pacific. Some of them came to share our meals for several weeks.

How did your son fit in?

He was ten when we arrived at Mills and did not speak a word of English. He went to a local school and a few weeks later became president of his class. It was an honorary title but we were worried about his studies. You see, there was a three-year gap between studies in France and those in the USA, and we feared he might lose the habit of concentration when being taught something he had already known about for a long time – algebra for example.

Fortunately, however, he never stopped drawing. We had noticed his interest in painting just before the war when the Prado Museum collection was exhibited in Geneva. We were staying in the mountains nearby and went to see the paintings. Daniel insisted we return to visit the exhibition. We tried to dissuade him, saying that Geneva was too far away, that we were in the mountains especially for him and so on, but he insisted so much that we finally gave way and to our great surprise he went immediately to the paintings that had impressed him on his first visit.

Was he interested in music?

He was very musical, gifted for the piano, but he did not want to study music. At Mills he was able to initiate himself in music by listening to it on the wireless every evening, in particular a programme presented by an excellent musicologist, Alfred Frankenstein. Daniel has remarkable taste and sure critical sense, and is perfectly capable of judging performances of his father's music.

What was Milhaud's reaction to this?

He was very happy to have a painter son and was very interested

Daniel's qualities. He admired his independence and his imagination. I appreciate most of all his essentially human qualities and his great goodness. These qualities came out during a terrible trial when he lost twenty years' work in a fire at the 'Bateau Lavoir' where he had his studio. He bore this disaster with a lot of courage and just carried on working. For some time now has devoted himself to sculpture.

Did Daniel take art lessons at Mills?

No, but as the son of a teacher he had the right to borrow books from the College library and he took full advantage of it. He did not have to follow classes in the history of art – he learned it on his own.

One day, I remember, Daniel quite astounded us. In our bedroom at Aix we had a little room that we had covered with engravings of ladies' fashions taken from a nineteenth-century magazine called *Le Journal des Demoiselles*. To my great surprise I found the copy of one of these engravings in a Woolworths store in Oakland. I bought it and gave it to Daniel. He looked at it with contempt, but after a moment, said that this engraving could have inspired a

17. Darius and Daniel, 1945

portrait that Cézanne painted of his mother and sister. Several weeks later the great Cézanne specialist Venturi came to see us and we told him about Daniel's discovery. He was amazed and we realized that Daniel had been right, which is very encouraging for doting parents!

Didn't he study with Dalí?

No, but we did meet Dalí in 1943 when he was staying in a hotel in Monterey. We told him our son was interested in painting and Dalí wanted to have a private chat with him. So he took Daniel off to his room while we awaited the end of the talk with some anxiety. We wondered what advice that notorious nonconformist could give our son. After a while, which seemed an eternity, Daniel came back: 'He told me I should draw every day'. Some years later he chose to study with Kokoschka, who was a master in the true sense of the word. He left him when he felt he had to fly with his own wings.

May we turn to your career now. Did you act on stage before your marriage?

No. I began to act in the thirties after my father's death. My mother was left without any money and I did not want Darius to have to help her on his own. So, as I had studied acting very seriously up to the age of fifteen, I hoped I could return to it and earn a living.

I had been surprised by the interest I had felt during the rehearsals at the Théâtre de l'Atelier, of which Charles Dullin was the director. There I had the feeling I understood much more clearly what was being asked for on the stage than I had ever done at an orchestral rehearsal. So I shyly asked Dullin if I could follow his classes: 'You're pretty small,' he said. I was tempted to reply but did not, 'And you, sir, are humpbacked.' He suggested I present a scene for an end-of-year audition. I worked like blazes and a few weeks later went along to present the final scene of Ibsen's *Doll's House*. Afterwards, Dullin smiled at me and said, 'Why not?' I made my début in Aristophanes' *The Birds*, for which Auric had written the incidental music, and I had to sing a song he had composed.

What sort of roles did you play?

As I was no longer particularly young I did not want to play the part of leading ladies. I was more attracted to character parts: nasty women, stupid women and such like!

What did Milhaud think of your new career?

I was a bit worried because Milhaud did not like to be left alone even for a short while. If I was a bit late in getting home he would fret and worry. So, as at that time he was working as a music critic, he got into the habit of coming to the theatre after the concert and waiting in my dressing room. Sometimes he brought some work with him. He never complained about my absences, and yet there were many of them because I was also working for the radio. The area I chose there was poetry reading and I was completely free to choose the texts. In those days there were very few poetry readings on French radio. I shared another programme with a young poet which featured recently published poetry. We made a point of including a poem from the past, scouring the anthologies to find ones that were generally unknown. I also organized programmes for schoolchildren and even did some advertising for a beauty cream. I was Mademoiselle Crème Simon, and received flowers from admirers! I gave drama classes at the Schola Cantorum two or three times a week. On occasion I participated in a number of concerts as a reciter. The work with the different composers was fascinating. I remember doing several Joan of Arcs, one by Manuel Rosenthal, another one by Roland Manuel, and I was also Schiller's Joan of Arc for Marseilles Radio, and during the war I did Péguy's Joan of Arc. The only one I never happened to act in was Honegger's!

Did you continue acting in America?

No, but all the same I couldn't entirely give up that side of my life. I started right away by producing plays in French with my students. I had no financial help so I dressed the students in pyjamas and assorted oddments – it's difficult to describe. The pawn shop was most useful! Milhaud's students of course provided the music.

18. *From left to right:* Daniel, Darius, Madeleine,
Charles Trenet, San Francisco, 1946

19. *Escape Me Never* (Margaret Kennedy), with
Georges Pitoëff (*left*), 1936

You also regularly attended the summer session in Aspen. Was there ever any conflict with Mills?

You're right, it eventually became impossible to combine the two. We chose to go to Aspen in summer because it really was a very special place. It was in fact a winter resort, but a Chicago industrialist, Walter Paepcke, had the idea of setting up a summer festival there, and a music school to go with it. It had a unique atmosphere. Aspen was a village of less than a thousand inhabitants; the streets had no names; the doors were always left open, day and night. We were soon adopted by the inhabitants. The butcher brought us trout (he loved fishing but detested fish!), and the grocer's wife brought us sweet peas because she knew I liked them. They contributed as much as possible in the activities of the festival. It was their thing in a way. Every summer I produced several operas with some professionals and students. I could borrow any props from them, even silverware. It was marvellous for several years. Then Aspen grew . . . and grew . . . It is still very successful. Darius had a composer invited every summer whose works were performed. The composer would talk about his work with the students. Among those who came were Virgil Thomson, Copland, Sessions, Chavez, Dallapiccola, Messiaen, Sauguet, etc.

What did you do in Aspen?

I taught drama and produced one-act operas, classical and contemporary. My aim was to develop the students' knowledge of different styles. Most of my students specialized in singing. And then, as the teachers were supposed to take part in the concerts, I had to do some reciting in a few cantatas – even in English, which terrified me! I read texts for works of the American composer Charles Jones. He had the patience to help me work at my pronunciation whenever necessary – and it always was. We had met Charles in 1940 at Mills. He taught there and we have kept in close contact ever since. His music is individual, refined, very attractive and unfortunately not well known enough.

Did you have other opportunities for reciting?

Yes, for example *Les Choéphores* in New York with Mitropoulos, but many other concerts as well. And then I made a few records. I also read poetry and drama in the course of countless lectures.

Did you perform with Milhaud?

In *Les Choéphores* before the war, with Milhaud conducting. After the performance, while we were acknowledging the applause, he gently caressed my face . . . instead of kissing my hand ceremoniously! He was always indulgent with me. All the same he certainly had no illusions. When he saw me rehearse a text for a long time he would gently say to me 'Stop it! You will always make mistakes, and never in the same place.' I was able to make plenty of mistakes, as we gave the *Cantate de l'Enfant et de la Mère* very many times.

And after his death?

I took part in concerts, especially abroad, but that chapter is now finished. However, I continue to give talks from time to time. I read poems for myself. It is a great joy – almost a necessity.

How did you manage to travel to Aspen every summer?

Aspen was exactly midway between Mills and New York, so we used to stop there on the way to France and on our way back to Mills the following year.

Why was there such a delay before your return to France after the war?

We needed petrol for the car, as Milhaud could not walk much, and we just had to be patient until 1947. We took a Norwegian cargo ship from San Francisco. What a joy it was to see the white cliffs of Dover! The boat made a 48-hour stop in Belgium. The Collaers met us in Rotterdam. In Le Havre we met my brother and his wife. It was deeply moving. Their son had been deported. He

20. Milhaud in Aspen, Colorado, 1956

21. *Top row, from left to right:* Charles Jones, Walter Susskind, Walter Piston; *front row:* Henri Sauguet, Milhaud, Olivier Messiaen, Aspen, 1962

22. Rehearsals with students in the garden at Aspen, 1960s

had been only sixteen years old.

In Paris we stayed for a few days with friends before going on to Aix. We had brought with us from America the necessaries for setting up home again, as our flat had been *literally* emptied during the occupation. Finding Aix again without his parents, who had died during the war, was truly painful for Darius, though fortunately they had not been deported. As for my mother, she had been able to hide with a former servant when the Germans occupied Provence, later finding refuge in the Ardèche until the end of the war. The country house in Aix that Darius loved so much had been occupied by the Germans, and, as I've already said, when he saw his 'L'Enclos' transformed – devastated – he declared he could never live there again.

All this emotion got the better of his health and he fell ill for a week. He was supposed to conduct his Third Symphony back in Paris. It includes a setting of the *Te Deum* and had been commissioned by the radio to celebrate the end of the war. Désormière conducted it in his place.

Milhaud was anxious to get back to Paris. He had agreed to teach composition at the Conservatoire, but in view of his state of health he received his pupils at home. Milhaud was extremely conscientious about his teaching duties. Although often ill, he never missed a class. If he went away on a trip, he made up for the lessons when he got back.

What was your Paris flat like when you returned after the war?

We were able to keep our flat thanks to Roger Désormière who took it upon himself to pay the rent for us throughout the war. When the Germans occupied Paris, he came with Sauguet to carry off the paintings and boxes full of important papers for safe keeping, depositing them with Honegger, who, as a Swiss citizen, was less likely to have his flat searched. Shortly afterwards the Germans did come. They took away all the music, all the books, etc. etc. and placed a portrait of Wagner on the piano! After that they left and sealed the door. The concierge took advantage of the situation, breaking the seals and moving out everything inside, and then declaring a burglary to the Gestapo.

Was she still there when you came back?

No, but in any case we did not have the intention of getting back all our property. We had survived the war, we had not suffered from hunger, from cold or from fear, and we did not want to take the law into our own hands, but we very quickly realized that for the sake of the people who had behaved properly during the occupation – even to the point of risking their lives – we were obliged to do something about it.

What did you do?

With the help of our faithful friend Henri Sauguet, I conducted a veritable detective enquiry. I did not have the address of the concierge, but I knew where her daughter's shop was. However, she was away ill in a sanatorium. I told the salesgirl that I knew Paulette had kept some things safe for us. Quite spontaneously she took us into the back room where we came across an armchair and our Directory cabinet. We asked where the concierge lived. It was near Fontainebleau. We went there right away. I cannot say that Madame G. was especially pleased to see me! She swore she had taken nothing from our flat, neither she nor her daughter.

So we registered an official complaint and several weeks later I returned to Madame G's with two police officers. I opened all the cupboards and found myself in the presence of our possessions, vases, plates, dishes and so forth. However, our furniture was nowhere to be seen; she had sold everything. We stashed everything we found into baskets, and just before leaving, Madame G. said to me 'At last, I shall have some space in my cupboards'!

I brought everything back to the flat where Milhaud was waiting impatiently for me. I started to open the boxes. I carefully put on the table a vase that Henri Hoppenot had brought us back from Persia. It was a very valuable object. The cat immediately broke it. A good lesson in philosophy, don't you think?

So, little by little, the flat began to take on a more human feeling. Before returning to France we had often wondered how we would be received by our friends who had undergone the Occupation. We very soon realized that Darius was awaited with impatience and affection by the whole musical fraternity.

The musicians who had played an important part in the Resistance had founded a little club called the 'Gloxinia' – the title of a song by Auric! The club was supposed to be secret, and nicknames were chosen for each member. Quite unexpectedly they asked Darius to become President of the 'Gloxinia' and called him 'Bolivar'.

So we used to go to their supper parties, which took place twice a month or so. I insist on the word 'we', because the club included female musicians, but in many cases not their husbands, if they were not musicians or had no link with the musical world. But you had to pass a test. I was fairly confident of passing, because I had found, in the complete works of Verlaine, a poem called 'Traversée' which I liked, and I had read it out to a number of artists and musicians and writers, and none of them had been able to guess the author. The members of 'Gloxinia' couldn't guess it either, so I passed, and they called me 'Le Colibri' – 'Humming Bird'.

May I ask who the other members of the 'Gloxinia' were, or is it still a secret?

I don't think so. There was Auric, Poulenc, Sauguet, Henri Barraud, Jane Bathori, Marcel Mihalovici, his wife Monique Haas, Irène Joachim, Désormière of course, and Jacques Rouché, the old ex-director of the Paris Opera, who had been invited on purpose as a gesture of sympathy after the way he had been removed from his post during the war.

What works did Milhaud have in hand at that time?

Darius composed a ballet on an argument by Jean Genet, *'Adame Miroir*, which was put on by Roland Petit. We were present at the first performance, as well as that of another ballet, *Jeux de Printemps*, at the Opéra Comique, but it was difficult for Milhaud to get about. He had not been able to attend any other musical events that had been proposed to him. There remained one, however, which was particularly important. He was supposed to conduct the première of his Fourth Symphony, written to celebrate the centenary of the Revolution of 1848. But how was he to do this in his state of health?

I remembered having seen Ysaÿe in Brussels being supported by two people who helped him reach the podium. This gave me the courage to ask Désormière if he would agree to rehearse the musicians, letting Milhaud conduct his symphony for the concert. Thus it was that Milhaud, in evening dress, crossed Paris in an ambulance on his way to the Champs Élysées Theatre, sitting next to the driver. Cars were still rare at that time, and such a sight left a curious impression on the passers-by! That was just a few days before we were to leave for the USA.

How was he able to travel?

Thanks to a wheelchair! It enabled us to undertake countless trips in circumstances that were often difficult but never insurmountable. On that occasion Milhaud had to give some master classes in Tanglewood for pupils of Copland before going on to the Music

23. Behind the scenes at the Festival Milhaud,
Long Beach, California, 1966

Academy of the West in Santa Barbara, where he had become honorary president, and finally on to Mills again for a year.

How could he absent himself so regularly from the Paris Conservatoire?

Milhaud had only accepted to teach there if he could retain his post at Mills. He'd been appointed to the Conservatoire through the earnest desire of the director, Claude Delvincourt. He was a minor composer who had been seriously wounded in the First World War, and he was an excellent director. During the Second World War he managed to hide or provide papers for all his students, and not one of them was taken for the labour camps in Germany. He was a stubborn man. He wrote to Milhaud immediately after the war saying, 'Darius, I need you. I need someone like you.' Milhaud did not want to give up Mills, so he proposed to Delvincourt that he teach in Paris every other year. This was not customary, but Delvincourt was a stubborn man, and managed to have the Ministry send Milhaud on a mission to the USA every second year! Meanwhile, Jean Rivier took over Milhaud's classes.

Did he find there was a difference between the students in the two countries?

Their mentality was different. The French students were less interested in their classmates' work than were the Americans. They were more independent.

Did you follow his classes?

Never. But I found it amusing every year to hear the same extracts from Mozart's Sonatas and an example taken from *Boris Godunov*. Milhaud used to emphasize the freedom and fantasy with which Mozart would introduce new ideas, and to demonstrate how

24. Milhaud with Charles Jones, arriving in California, 1948

horrible Rimsky-Korsakov's orchestration of Mussorgsky's opera was and how it completely betrayed the composer's intentions.

Some of them were also students of Messiaen?

Yes! He was a wonderful teacher and had a great influence on all his pupils.

What about Milhaud's influence?

I do not know whether a teacher who refused all systems and who had no philosophical or other theory to deliver could impress his students. It was only after quite a few years that they appreciated his spirit of independence and his contempt for 'followers'. But a former student told me, 'I never saw Milhaud angry, except once, when one of us brought him a piece which looked like his own music.'

And what about the twelve-tone system?

He didn't actually have any pupils who were dodecaphonists. On the other hand, if some of them wanted to follow Boulez's classes, Milhaud always encouraged them to do this, so long as they described to him what they learned, as it interested him.

Darius, like Schönberg for that matter, thought one should never use serial technique before having acquired a non-serial technique. This was true also for electronic music. In the early fifties Darius proposed that Mills College buy the electronic studio and equipment of a former pupil of his, Morton Subotnick, as he was leaving for New York. Darius thought the material should be made available for students on the condition that they first master traditional techniques.

Was his advice followed?

Not always!

Were Milhaud's pupils interested in the music of his own generation?

On the whole, no, which is perhaps natural enough. However, some of his American pupils were interested in the music of Satie. In the fifties and sixties, a period of 'happenings' and repetitive music, Satie was seen by young composers as something of a pioneer.

You did of course know Satie personally, but let me ask you when Milhaud first met him.

When he came back from Brazil in 1919. Strangely enough it was in Rio that he got to know Satie's music. He became friends with the musicians, the Guerras, who possessed all Satie's works and so admired his music that they even called their dog 'Satie'. Ever since the first performance of *Parade*, a number of young composers had grouped around Satie.

Why did they call him 'the Good Fairy'?

Because they knew he was interested in them, that he was always keen to get to know their music. Darius had been very struck by Satie's attitude towards young people and perhaps it influenced him as a teacher.

How did they get on together?

Very well. They had a lot in common, for example, their attitudes towards audiences and critics. They were the only composers as far as I know who were utterly indifferent to what people, especially critics, thought of their music.

What was Satie like as a man?

He looked like a solicitor's clerk from the 1910s: a pince-nez, tiny, mischievous little eyes, a beard that was always impeccably cut. He spoke slowly, breaking the syllables up. His delivery seemed artificial, in contradiction with what he said, which was spontaneous.

He would put his hand in front of his mouth when he laughed. In fact this man, whose thoughts were the epitome of the anti-bourgeois, was dressed just like one with his dark suit and bowler hat.

And umbrella of course!

Yes! Don't forget his mother was British. Perhaps that also accounts for the bowler hat!

We know that he had an early love-affair with the painter Suzanne Valadon, the mother of Utrillo. Did he ever talk about her?

No, never! I think he had been very deeply in love with her, but Satie's personal life was always secret. It was impossible to guess whether he had a love-life.

And what about his character?

He was extremely polite, but would suddenly blow up for no reason that seemed logical to us. His attitude was sometimes surprising, unexpected. There was the episode of the singer who was giving a very bad rendition of his songs, but that just amused him enormously. On the other hand, one day when he was playing the piano and had asked Sauguet to turn the pages and one was turned just a bit late, Satie flew into a terrible rage and did not speak to Sauguet for several days.

When his ballet *Mercure* was performed for the first time, the spectacle was disturbed by a violent demonstration by the Surrealists. We were in Satie's box. The whistling and shouting hardly touched him at all. He looked at his watch, stood up and calmly left the box to be in good time to catch the last train. But the public's attitude during the performance of his 'furniture music' incensed him.

What happened?

Satie thought that music could be treated as decoration, in the same way as wallpaper in the house. In other words, music that is played but not listened to. The experiment took place during the interval between the two halves of a concert in an art gallery. As soon as the audience heard the music they stopped talking and went back to their seats. Satie was furious and shouted to them, 'Keep talking! Walk about!' Hardly a success; the experiment had failed. And yet, not quite! Is not 'furniture music' imposed everywhere today? . . . In supermarkets, lifts, planes. Contrary to what one might think, some of his actions which seemed incongruous were in fact logical.

What about his candidature to the Institute when he was a young man?

The tendency is to choose people for the Institute who are already old. Would it not be more logical to appoint young academicians? Satie had an extremely youthful spirit. He was always surprising us – as he did in those little texts in so many of his piano pieces, the humour of the texts attenuating the classicism of the actual music. Was this out of shyness or modesty? I shall never know. I must say, however, that he would have been furious to learn that some people read out his texts in public. In Aspen once, I was asked to read the texts in *Sports et Divertissements* during a performance. I at first refused but eventually had to oblige as faculty members were supposed to take part in the festival's activities. The result was that the texts were greatly appreciated and the music not at all!

In the middle of his ballet *Relâche*, René Clair's film *Entr'acte* was shown. Satie did not just compose the music for the whole spectacle, he agreed to take part in the film. One can see dear Satie with his umbrella on the terrace on the Champs Élysées Theatre, apparently jumping over the edge. And at the end of the performance Satie surprised us by coming to take a bow in Désormière's little car! He was accompanied by Picabia who had designed the décors. That is what I called a youthful, fantastical mind.

When did he fall ill?

Shortly after *Relâche*. He had got into the habit of coming to have lunch with us twice a week. He would stay for the whole afternoon.

The other days he would go to Braque's or Derain's, but as he became weaker and weaker we decided he really could not go back to Arcueil. With Jean Wiéner we set him up in a comfortable room in a hotel, but he hated it! He sat all day in front of the mirror on the back of the wardrobe door looking at himself. He had a string attached to his armchair and to the door so he would not have to get up to open it. He looked utterly gloomy. After two days, he vanished. We tracked him down to a little hotel in Montparnasse frequented by artists' models. There he was, lying on the bed with a high temperature. We got a doctor who said Satie had to go straight to hospital. Thanks to the Count de Beaumont we were able to have a private room in the Saint Joseph hospital. I began to pack Satie's suitcase. I have never been good at packing, so I asked Braque, who was a large man, to stand between Satie and the suitcase so he could not see what I was doing. We of course accompanied him to his hospital room. When the ambulance crossed a square where there was a celebrated *brasserie* Satie said to us 'What if we go and have a drink?' It was, alas, because he had drunk too much that we were taking him to the hospital, for he had cirrhosis of the liver.

When the nurse, who was a nun, had unpacked his suitcase, she asked me for some soap. Satie did not have any. He used a pumice stone, 'like the ancient Chinese', as he said. It was no doubt very effective. He was always absolutely clean and his skin was extremely soft.

He gave me a mark of confidence which greatly touched me. He asked me to go and fetch some linen from Arcueil. So I went there and saw the miserable building in which he lived. The concierge handed me the bundle and I left without asking any questions, though I should very much have liked to do so. Satie at once had a look at what I had brought back. He counted the handkerchiefs. Two were missing – there were only eighty-six! Unhappily, his state of health got no better. We should have liked to inform a member of his family. His sister was in the Argentine, he did not know where. As for his brother, he 'never wanted to see him again after what he had done . . .', as he said. Immediately after Satie's death Darius put a notice in several newspapers and shortly afterwards Satie's brother and his nephew, both carrying umbrellas, came to see Darius. Conrad was extremely friendly, very much attached to his brother even though they had stopped seeing each other a long time before for some utterly futile reason. He entrusted Darius with the task of sorting out the manuscripts which we found in his bedroom and which he had thought were lost. Conrad gave the letters and articles and manuscripts to Milhaud, who in turn, just before World War II, gave them to the Bibliothèque Nationale, only keeping those he had acquired during Satie's lifetime. The unfortunate man was often in need of money. He certainly could not have foreseen that twenty years later his music would become so popular and that the *Gymnopédies* would be played all over the place, even as radio and television credits.

Sometimes in Debussy's orchestration?

No, unfortunately. And I regret it, as it is a mark of the admiration Debussy had for Satie. They were close friends for more than thirty years. Ravel also was one of his admirers. Is not 'La Belle et la Bête', from *Ma Mère l'Oye*, a *Gymnopédie*?

What was Milhaud's relationship with Ravel?

They met many times at the homes of common friends. At the Godebskis' first of all. They received regularly, every Sunday evening. They were exceptionally cordial and kind hosts. We would come across Ricardo Viñes there, Jane Bathori, Satie, and Ravel. Ravel was very devoted to them, and to their two children. It was for them indeed that he wrote *Ma Mère l'Oye*.

Ravel also frequented the salon of Jeanne Dubost; a charming, elegant, whimsical woman who liked to surround herself with artists and writers. We would meet at her place every Wednesday afternoon. Music was often played. We were entertained by Oboukhov, by Horowitz, just arrived from Russia, and above all by a Red Indian chief who sang at the top of his voice and jumped all over the place! To thank our hostess for her hospitality, a few composers such as Ravel, Schmitt, Honegger, Milhaud and some others each composed a little piece which was performed, to her great surprise, in her salon. Jacques Rouché, the director of the

Paris Opera, was present at this friendly event and proposed making a spectacle from these pieces called *L'Eventail de Jeanne* ('Jeanne's Fan'). To be introduced to the Opera with a polka did not give Milhaud much pleasure.

What kind of person was Ravel?

I did not know him well enough to be able to speak of him at length, but there can be no doubt he had a kind and generous disposition and he gave proof of moral courage as well. He could not help knowing that Milhaud was not an unconditional admirer of his music, yet this never influenced his behaviour towards him. He even spoke of Darius with admiration in the course of his lectures in the USA. Indeed he threatened to withdraw from a Music Committee in Paris if Milhaud were refused admittance. I think he appreciated some works of Darius. I can still see myself going up the Champs Élysées arm in arm with him after the first performance of *Les Malheurs d'Orphée*, which he particularly liked. We were not close friends but had harmonious relations with him. He came to lunch with us once, just a family occasion. Daniel was very young and was standing on his bed. He had been struck by Ravel's height – he was not very tall – and greeted him by saying 'Hello, old friend!' Ravel was delighted!

A few weeks later Ravel conducted one of his works at the Salle Pleyel. Darius went to congratulate him after the concert, asking him to sign an autograph for Daniel. Ravel took his pen, held it for a long moment before murmuring, 'I can't write my own name down'. It was the start of that cruel illness that tortured him until his death, for he was quite aware of his condition, and we saw him much less frequently in the salons or at friends' receptions.

Did you like to go out to the salons?

I was certainly less '*mondaine*' than Milhaud. In fact, neither of us was keen on parties, but there were some places that were fascinating as they gave one the opportunity of seeing old friends or meeting foreign artists who were stopping over in Paris. It was the case with the Sunday afternoons at Paul Clémenceau's, the brother of the statesman, whose wife was Viennese. German and Austrian artists were always welcome to her home. She knew a lot of artists as her father was head of an important newspaper in Vienna. I had the pleasure of meeting Arthur Schnitzler there.

Were they also patrons of the arts?

No, they were not. They were content just to provide unforgettable Viennese delicacies. I do however have a very vivid memory of the Kolisch Quartet playing Beethoven by heart completely in the dark, with just a fire burning in the chimney! On the other hand the Count de Beaumont and Charles de Noailles were patrons, and I must not forget the Princess de Polignac. She liked to have works performed that she had herself commissioned, *Socrate*, for example, *Renard, Les Malheurs d'Orphée*. It was there that I heard *El Retablo de Maese Pedro*. It was a very striking spectacle.

Was De Falla present?

Yes. He came to Paris quite often. In his youth he had spent several years here and had numerous friends, but you had to meet him in

25. Masked ball given by Count Étienne de Beaumont,
Paris, 1922: Milhaud centre, wearing the wig

Granada, in his 'domain'. He received us there with extreme kindness. He took us to visit the Alhambra, the Generalife and also the gypsy quarter, which teemed with people, singers, children, beggars . . . Falla knew what visitors had to expect in this area, and so when a beggar accosted him he brought out a special empty wallet from his pocket, and then went on his way. Falla surprised us by coming unannounced to visit us in the country. We were leaving the next day for Portugal and so were unable to take him round Aix. Then the war separated us, and we never saw him again.

Was it out of friendship that Milhaud dedicated *Christophe Colomb* to De Falla?

When Darius was composing *Colomb*, he heard that Falla was writing his *Atlantide* and he was afraid Christopher Columbus might be an important figure in that opera. De Falla reassured him that Columbus had only a secondary role. Nonetheless, as a mark of friendship, Darius dedicated his opera to him.

Coming back to patrons, what about Mrs Coolidge?

You're right. She was a generous patron. There was something special about her, something which made her different from the others: she was almost completely deaf! She would sit alone in the front row with an ear trumpet that had several wires dangling from it. You would go up to her during a concert with a certain trepidation; she was rather frightening. But she had an entirely disinterested love of music and she helped numerous musicians. When Darius arrived at Mills in July 1940 his salary could not be budgeted for, as such expenses are planned months in advance. Mrs Coolidge spontaneously paid his first year's salary. She subsidized the Pro Arte Quartet for their first tour in 1927; she commissioned various works for them, including three quartets from Darius. Mrs Coolidge was thoroughly independent and seemed deaf to any influences.

Did Milhaud ever receive a commission from England?

In 1933 a charming aesthete, Edward James, organized a ballet sea-on for his wife, the dancer Tilly Losch, and commissioned *The Seven Deadly Sins* from Kurt Weill, *Fastes* from Henri Sauguet and *Les Songes* from Milhaud. This ballet had the particularity that the painter Derain was responsible for the scenario as well as the décors and costumes.

Did you know any English composers? Lord Berners perhaps, who is sometimes referred to as an English member of Les Six?

I never knew him, but Darius knew him and told me he used to travel around with a harpsichord in his car boot all the time! I did however have the pleasure of meeting Constant Lambert at Aix when he came to see Darius. His culture and intelligence were remarkable. It is a pity I did not get to know him better.

Arthur Bliss was teaching at Berkeley during the war and lived not far from us. We did not know him and his wife but they had the kindness to invite us to share their Thanksgiving dinner. We were especially moved by the warmth and generosity of their hospitality. Unfortunately we lost sight of them after their return to England.

Humphrey Searle was among the composers invited to the Summer Sessions at Aspen. I produced his opera *The Diary of a Madman*. He appeared satisfied with it, as did his wife, and we saw them again in London, and even in Geneva where they surprised us by coming to wish Milhaud well on his eightieth birthday.

I suppose in view of his reputation in the twenties we ought to have met Walton, but never did. Darius and I liked his *Façade* very much indeed. In fact I was mad with jealousy, as it is exactly the kind of text I should like to have recited, but my English was not quite good enough. I am not an Edith Sitwell! By the way, have you ever realized that *Façade* is an ancestor of rap? It has just the same sort of rhythmic relationship between the words and the music.

Did you know Britten?

We made his acquaintance at Aspen.

26. Milhaud with Benjamin Britten, Aspen, 1964

Did Milhaud like his music?

On the whole, yes, but he did wish his works would sometimes be a bit more daring! Indeed in the course of a lecture Britten declared that a composer should please the public. That was far removed from Milhaud's attitude and it shocked him.

Did Milhaud go to London often after the war?

Darius was invited several times by the BBC and conducted some of his works. We took advantage of one of these trips to see an excellent performance of *Les Troyens*, a work that had never been played in its entirety in France! It was a great joy for Milhaud to hear the whole of this work as he adored the music of Berlioz.

Was surprise in music something that Milhaud valued?

Most certainly. Yet he did not think surprise should be a mere 'effect'; just as he had no sympathy for followers who would undergo influences without trying to develop their own personality.

Was Milhaud interested in folk music?

He proved it in many works, and not just French folk music, but Brazilian, Latin American, American, Palestinian, even English if you count *The Beggar's Opera*! He thought that if one borrowed folk tunes or music from the past one should do something utterly personal and new with it. This is what he admired in the music of Bartók, de Falla, Stravinsky. It's interesting to note that contemporary composers such as Berio and Ligeti are interested in folk music.

What was Milhaud's view of Berio?

He was one of the young composers whom Milhaud admired the most, one of the few who had a gift for lyricism. Being ostracized by younger composers never bothered Milhaud, but he did feel that Berio was rather more broadminded than many others. Berio showed this by dedicating his *Passaggio* to Darius and by conducting *L'Homme et son Désir* and *La Mort du Tyran* in a concert organized shortly after Milhaud's death by Jean-Louis Barrault. Paul Méfano had agreed to recruit the players and in order to honour Milhaud's memory he brought together thirty or so composers who sang in the chorus of *La Mort du Tyran*.

Did Stockhausen study with Milhaud?

He had applied to study at the Paris Conservatoire and had to take an exam, but he made mistakes in the music dictation. Despite that, Darius wanted to take him in his class but the director of the

Conservatoire, Delvincourt, categorically refused to admit him. Darius insisted, but to no avail. We met him several years later after a concert at Mills College. We invited him to dinner and I was amused when he leafed through a score of Darius's which was on the piano and said 'It's funny one can still write music like this . . .'

Dallapiccola visited us some time after that.

Did Milhaud like his music?

He greatly admired his works. Although influenced by Schönberg, his music was very different from that of Schönberg's adepts. There is nothing gloomy in his music, even though he often dealt with serious subjects. He transports us into a world of light that is all his own.

Did Milhaud know any other Italian composers?

Casella, Malipiero, Castelnuovo-Tedesco, and especially Vittorio Rieti. His music is quite different. He was still very young when Darius met him in Rome and Rieti played his *Barabau* for him. Darius was so enthusiastic that he spoke about it to Diaghilev when he got back to Paris. This was the start of the collaboration between Rieti and the Ballets Russes. Rieti has written numerous ballet scores since then, always elegant, fresh, lively. He died recently at the age of ninety-six, composing right up to the end!

And Messiaen?

That takes me back to before the war, to the 'Jeune France' concerts. It was without a doubt his music that attracted the attention of Milhaud. When we came back to France in 1947 Messiaen was extremely famous, the uncontested and incontestable master of the music world. On the occasion of Darius's seventieth birthday, the director of the Aspen Festival proposed to him that he invite two composers. Darius chose Messiaen and Sauguet. Their presence contributed to the success of the celebrations, which were particularly brilliant. The inhabitants of Aspen had organized all sorts of games in order to raise the money for founding a bursary for a student which would carry Darius's name.

And Boulez?

For several years Boulez used to conduct incidental music for Jean-Louis Barrault. Indeed it was in his theatre that the first Domaine Musical concerts took place. He was a very conscientious conductor of the scores that were put before him, including the incidental music Darius wrote for *Le Livre de Christophe Colomb*. He had all the more merit in that he can hardly have appreciated such scores! When Milhaud's health allowed it, we attended the Domaine Musical concerts with a lot of interest.

Apart from the instance you mention, did Boulez ever conduct Milhaud's music?

Certainly not! I suppose he was and is completely allergic to it. This had no influence on Milhaud's opinion of Boulez's music. Moreover Milhaud had an extremely broad mind, which meant he was quite capable of being sympathetic to varied artistic tendencies.

And Sauguet?

He had written to Milhaud just after the First World War, when he was still living with his parents in Bordeaux. Darius invited him to spend a few days in Paris with him and attend some concerts. He presented Sauguet to all his musician friends. Not without difficulty, Sauguet managed to come and live in Paris a few months later. He adopted us and we adopted him. Milhaud was charmed by his musical qualities, his sensitivity, the elegance of his style and his personality. He had the gift of amusing Darius and cheering him up. Many times when Darius was in pain and low spirited, I telephoned Henri to ask him to come round. He would at once rush over and the miracle took place: I would hear Milhaud splitting his sides with laughter! Darius liked Sauguet's music very much. He attended all the performances of his opera *La Chartreuse de Parme*, based on Stendhal's novel. It is a superb work and at times achieves a stunning gravity. The score is dedicated to us, and I'm very proud of the fact.

Do the dedications of Milhaud's works have particular significance?

They reveal of course the relationship between the composer and the dedicatee. In many instances the dedicatee is the virtuoso who had commissioned the work. Sometimes it stems from the desire to evoke the memory of someone who had died. I do not want to make a list of such people but I shall mention Poulenc, for example, for whom Milhaud felt very great tenderness, almost a fraternal feeling. His unexpected death had profoundly upset Darius. Honegger's death was not such a surprise as he had never got over his heart attack of 1947, but their close relationship had never ceased and the subtitles of the string quintet that Milhaud wrote in Honegger's memory (his fourth) bear witness to his feelings: 'Lamentation on the death of a friend', 'Memories of youth', 'The sweetness of a long friendship', 'Hymn of praise'.

And yet Milhaud had reservations about Le Roi David?

He was not the only one! He felt Honegger's characteristics were somewhat lacking in this work, and that it happened when his music ought still to have been developing. It was a concession to the public. Of course as such it was a complete success, and still is today. The public was happy to have the impression of at last being able to appreciate contemporary music. It gave rise to something of a war between the 'Honeggerians' and the 'Milhaudists'. Fortunately the friendly relationship between Arthur and Darius was rock-solid and neither of them attached any importance to this situation. Even their wives were not affected by it, which is rather exceptional! Besides, we were always very close. Arthur and his wife often came to stay for a few days with us at Aix. Arthur was for me a true comrade. He lived not far from us in Paris, on the same boulevard in fact, and right up until the end of his life he would come over to spend some time with Milhaud. During his last years it was terrible to see him become so weakened, especially as he had been the incarnation of health and strength when he was young.

27. Madeleine as reciter, Darius as conductor in *Cantate de l'Enfant et de la Mère*, Toronto, 1951

Did you record some of his works?

I did his *Judith* in Salt Lake City with Abravanel and the Witch of Endor in *Le Roi David*. It is not a role that suits me at all, but at that time there were very few French reciters in the USA.

You also recorded some of Milhaud's works.

Two. One was a cantata on texts by Maurice Carême written for the tenth anniversary of the Pro Arte Quartet, *Cantate de l'Enfant et de la Mère*, the other a *Suite de Quatrains* with texts by Francis Jammes.

Milhaud also dedicated a number of works to you.

He was obliged to do so! Some works have to do with the theatre; then there is his Thirteenth String Quartet, because the number 13 has always been lucky, and the Sixteenth for our twentieth wedding anniversary. He even wrote a work in secret from me, hiding it from view whenever he heard me coming back home. It was a suite of fifteen pieces for piano called *The Household Muse*, dedicated to M.M.M.M. which stands for 'Madeleine Milhaud Muse Ménagère' – 'Madeleine Milhaud Household Muse'. These pieces are an illustration of our daily life and activities. From 'Poetry' to 'Tidying up the house', from 'Flowers in the house' to 'The kitchen', 'Laundry' and 'Delightful evenings'. Darius's opera *Bolivar* is dedicated to 'Swanee': that is what he called me since his stay in the USA in 1922.

You wrote the libretto for this opera. How many did you write in all?

Three, but you have to realize I am not a writer and unfortunately never shall be. It was a particular set of circumstances that led me to write these librettos. In 1938 Darius had received a State commission and wanted to compose an opera. He simply had to find a text. He had often expressed his feelings as far as jealousy was concerned, considering it the greatest proof of love that can be given to the loved one. Medea was an obvious figure for this. The idea appealed to Milhaud who at once began to write to friends who might be able to prepare a libretto. Unfortunately they were all on holiday and Milhaud was impatient. So, he turned to me. I refused! But he insisted to such an extent that I gave in. I borrowed extracts from here and there in Medeas by Seneca, Euripides and Corneille, and above all prepared a libretto by taking into account Milhaud's style.

The first performance of the opera took place in Antwerp at the start of the war. The performance at the Paris Opera was planned for March 1940. Darius had been ill for a month in Aix and was incapable of travelling there. It was then that a policeman effected a miracle! We had blacked out all our window panes, but we did not know that Daniel had scratched 'Down with Hitler' on every one of them with the point of a pair of scissors. We were at fault of course, and a policeman came along to fine us. With an air of authority he went upstairs to our bedroom. He asked Milhaud why he was confined to his bed, and without losing a second proceeded to give him a séance of magnetism! Believe it or not, two days later, we drove to Paris and were able to attend the première of *Médée* at

he Paris Opera. It was a memorable evening! A superb perfor-
aance, though we heard the continual sound of the anti-aircraft
uns. The Germans had invaded Holland and were continuing their
ffensive in the direction of Belgium. Our friend Henri Hoppenot,
ho worked in the Foreign Ministry, insisted that we return imme-
iately to Aix. France was invaded in its turn a few weeks later, and
ur exile commenced . . .

Darius's mind was constantly preoccupied by the evolution of
ae war. He awaited the liberation with anxiety and impatience. I
old you how Darius came to write an opera on Simón Bolívar, the
berator of slaves, the man who threw off the Spanish yoke from
outh America. Well, the author of the play, Jules Supervielle, was
a Montevideo at the time and Darius asked him to authorize me

28. 'The Household Muse', Mills College, 1945

to prepare a libretto from his play. He accepted, and also accepte
the task of writing 'airs' wherever necessary for the action.
respected his text, just shortening it here and there and sometime
changing the order of the scenes. All the same, I did feel the nee
to introduce a genuine text of Bolívar's into my libretto, and to tha
end extracted a passage from his will, which is an astounding tex

**Was Milhaud at all demanding when you prepared a libretto fo
him? Did he ask you to change things?**

Very rarely. He was conscious of the fact that I did the job solel
to help him.

La Mère coupable was our last collaboration. The work is base
on the third play in Beaumarchais' trilogy. It features the sam
characters as The Barber of Seville and The Marriage of Figaro, bu
older now and more reasonable. Beaumarchais introduced a villai
into the play, a diabolical creature who is prepared to destro
everything for his own profit. However, his ploys are thwarted b
Figaro and the highly complicated imbroglio which almost turns t
drama ends in joy. It was very well staged in Geneva.

**It seems to me that a number of first performances of Milhaud
operas took place abroad.**

You're right! Especially in Germany, where two of his most impor
tant works were first performed: L'Orestie and Christoph
Colomb.

Is Milhaud's music much performed in Israel?

Less than you might imagine! Israel is mainly associated in m
mind with the first performance of his opera David. It wa
Koussevitzky who took the initiative of asking him to write a wor
for the celebration of the three thousandth anniversary of th
founding of Jerusalem. Before setting to work Darius wished t
visit Israel to absorb the atmosphere of the country. We went wit
Armand Lunel who had agreed to write the libretto, which, in view
of the scope and diversity of the subject, was not easy! Interestingl

e were received in Israel with a certain distrust as our names did ot strike the Israelis as being properly Jewish; they were used to olish or German names. Moreover they had been shocked by an merican film, Henry King's 1951 epic *David and Bathsheba*, star- ng Gregory Peck and Susan Hayward, which went into great etail about David's love affairs with Bathsheba, and they were fraid of an opera written by two Frenchmen! On that point at least unel was able to reassure them. He prepared a remarkable bretto, portraying the most important events in the life of the ing, some of which of course were very dramatic. Darius sug- ested that he take advantage of his stay in Israel to audition ingers, as he wanted to perform the opera with Israelis, deliber- tely writing the chorus parts for amateurs. Only the role of David equired a professional singer. It made a great impression on Darius to be composing an opera in honour of a hero whose mem- ry was constantly present in Israel. In travelling around the coun- ry we were struck by the fact that many of the places mentioned 1 the biblical story of David were also places where the Israelis and ritish had fought in the recent conflict. It was this that gave Darius he idea of having two choruses in the opera, one representing the sraelites of old, the other present-day Israelis.

The performance in Jerusalem was unforgettable for us. We had he impression the public became one with the action. It was their istory that was being sung, their Jerusalem that was being cele- rated. When we left Jerusalem the next morning Darius was ailed and fêted as he arrived at the airport. We realized then that 1ost Israelis had heard the opera on the radio.

Several months later, at La Scala in Milan, the atmosphere was uite different. It became an admirably staged opera in a real the- tre, with the usual audience of season-ticket holders who had come o see whatever spectacle was being proposed that evening. A year ater *David* took on the character of a pageant. It was staged in the pen-air theatre of the Hollywood Bowl before 20,000 spectators!

s it the only opera by Milhaud to have a religious character?

Dne to do with the Old Testament, yes. However his last opera, *aint Louis, roi de France*, has a spiritual aspect on account of the main figure, and *Esther de Carpentras* of course deals with a religious community, though in a tragi-comic manner.

Milhaud was religious, then?

Yes, profoundly. He had a blind faith.

What do you mean by blind?

I mean that he was faithful to the religion of his ancestors without ever posing the slightest question. His religious feelings come out very clearly, I think, if you listen to his religious works. If you listen closely to his *Sacred Service* I feel his humility comes out, his relationship with his Creator. A lot of his works are like this, especially cantatas and choral pieces.

Yes, I'm struck by the diversity of the sources of inspiration for his cantatas.

You're right. Some are liturgical, some have to do with human passions, with the human condition – for which Darius felt profound pity or even terror, as in *Le Château du Feu* which sets a poignant text by Jean Cassou describing the horrors of the holocaust. *La Tragédie humaine*, which has a text by Agrippa d'Aubigny, deplores the wrongs of wars waged in the name of religion. It was the diversity within Milhaud's own character that led him to choose texts of very different natures. He even chose the text of Pope John XXIII, the encyclical *Pacem in Terris* which recommends ecumenism in the Christian Church and the right to honour God according to one's own conscience. It condemns racism, the distress of political refugees, the arms race. How can one not be impressed by such a far-reaching text?

Contrary to what a large part of the public thinks, composers feel free to go down quite varied paths. The essential thing is to believe in what you express. For example Darius wrote a *Te Deum* in 1946 as part of his Third Symphony as well as a *Sacred Service* (from Jewish liturgy) in 1948.

ut how does one actually set an encyclical to music?

arius first obtained the authorization of the Vatican, especially
 one is not normally allowed to make cuts in a papal text. Then
e made his own selection of extracts of the encyclical, parts that
rresponded to his deeply held beliefs, and organized them as
los, recitations and choral items. In order to underline the ecu-
enical nature of the work – and at the express demand of the
atican – its first performance was conducted by a Protestant,
harles Münch. Moreover the score was published by Madame
labert, who was an Orthodox Christian. The oratorio was pre-
ièred for the inauguration of the main auditorium of the Maison
 la Radio in Paris and was also given a few weeks later in Notre-
ame, which was then celebrating its eight hundredth anniver-
ry. However, the liberal ideas of John XXIII were not
ppreciated by everyone and when *Pacem* was performed in San
rancisco, a lady came up to Milhaud saying 'How did you dare
t the text of a red pope?'!

was not through any political commitment that he wrote such
orks?

o. He was too independent minded to subject himself to the
emands of a political party, whatever it might be, just as he
ever shut himself up in a system of composition. Indeed religion
d his ongoing work were the only two areas in which he never
lt free.

d he take an interest in current affairs?

bsolutely. He followed events very regularly. It was impossible
r him to remain indifferent with regard to certain things, so some
 his works do deal with what you might call 'political affairs'. *La
ort du Tyran*, for example, the text of which, by Lampridius,
scribes how an angry crowd murders a tyrant.

Where were Milhaud's sympathies during the time of the student riots in 1968?

With the students, of course. They had a lot to complain about and still have, unfortunately.

What were his relationships with his own students like?

Absolutely excellent. A large number of them are still faithful, and I had a proof of their loyalty just after he died. One of his pupils Kathy Warne, has even created a Milhaud association in the USA which she runs in a very dynamic way, with great tenacity and love

How was Milhaud able to organize his time. Wasn't it awkward for him to interrupt his composition in order to teach?

In fact it was the other way round. He would set to work as soon as his classes were over, and he would interrupt his work towards the end of the afternoon to go for a trip out, or to see a film. In any case Milhaud never had any difficulty about settling down to work. He could work anywhere. He never worked at night, except when he had to finish a piece, but if he didn't have any classes, he would begin around 10 o'clock and then he would often work all day. I've seen him orchestrating a whole day long. He would never take a day's holiday. One day I went to the doctor with him and said, state this in front of a witness, if you don't take a few days' holiday I'm going to divorce you.' He didn't take me seriously, I'm afraid

He had no fads then, when composing?

He used to say 'All I need is ink in my fountain pen.' The shape of the table did not matter. In fact sometimes I saw him with manu script paper on his knees. He had great powers of concentration and noise never bothered him.

Did he use a sketch book?

Never. Very occasionally he noted rhythms in the margins of a page f text or on detached sheets of paper, but hardly ever actual itches. I didn't know this about his sketches during his lifetime. I ound it afterwards, because I never poked my nose into Milhaud's works. That's how we lived together in such a harmonious manner! I think nothing is worse than to live with someone who's always asking 'What are you doing? Is it going all right?' He didn't eed any help.

id he compose orchestral works directly into full score?

most cases, yes. Sometimes – and practically always in the case f works with voices – he would write what he called a 'first manuscript' for piano, though he never composed actually at the piano.

id he believe in inspiration?

y that, do you mean the breath that flows through any creation? Certainly in Milhaud's case it could be born from very varied ources: the death of a friend, the assassination of President Kennedy, his parents' golden wedding anniversary . . . a catalogue f agricultural machinery! Moreover he enjoyed solving difficult echnical problems. After all, who obliged him to write his ourteenth and Fifteenth String Quartets in such a way that they ould also be played simultaneously as an octet? Similarly he was ascinated by chance music – long before Cage and company. In 920 he wrote a piece for three clarinets to a text which was simly a cocktail recipe – the work was published in the *Almanac de Cocagne*. Musical phrases of different lengths are repeated ad libitum by the performers. When the singer has finished, the players ome to the end of their phrases, holding the last note until everyne has finished. Darius used this technique a lot in the sixties and eventies, most often writing the various melodic lines in different eys and different tempi!

You can also see his inventiveness in his pioneering use of the ercussion, even before Varèse. The position of the percussionist as changed so much over the past few decades that it is difficult believe that the soloist for the première of the Percussion Concerto in 1930 was so nervous about appearing in the limelight that he backed out at the last minute! Nowadays any budding percussionist can perform the work. I have often seen it performed by heart by fourteen-year-olds in America! It's interesting too that whereas in *L'Homme et son Désir* seventeen players were originally needed to deal with the percussion, it can be rearranged, as Bruce Mather has recently shown, for only six.

Learning your *métier* not only gives you freedom, as I've already said, but allows you to write a piece even at very short notice and treat it as a duty rather than a burden. For example, President Kennedy is murdered on a Thursday; on Friday Darius receives a phone call from America: 'Can you write a piece that we can perform next Wednesday?' If you like, shock is a form of inspiration.

On the other hand, you should not think that Darius always wrote on commission. Far from it! To give just a couple of examples, most of his string quartets and his operas were written entirely without commission. He wrote them simply because he wanted to.

Was Milhaud inspired by the timbre of particular instruments? Did he have a favourite instrument?

No, but he had some unfavourite instruments, the organ for example, and the harpsichord. Yet that did not prevent him from writing effectively for those instruments; perhaps they were a stimulus and challenge for him. He did not much care either for the traditionally soulful, melancholic way of writing for the cello, so when he wrote his first concerto for that instrument, he cocked a snook at the style by starting off with a very lackadaisical theme.

It is a legend that Milhaud composed extraordinarily quickly. Was it true?

On the whole he did write quickly, but you must understand that he would think about a work for a long time before actually starting to write it. He endeavoured to find the style that would suit a particular work. You know, it always amuses me when people express astonishment at the number of works Darius wrote. When

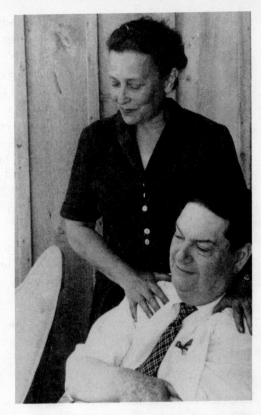

29. Darius and Madeleine, 1968

ou think that Schubert wrote more than 600 works between the
ges of fifteen and thirty, or Villa-Lobos more than a thousand, I
hink, what is so exceptional about the 450 or so works written by
omeone who died at the age of eighty-two?

Vhat did he see as the purpose of music?

am not quite sure he would have understood your question. No
oubt he would simply have replied that he composed because he
ould not do anything else.

Was he receptive to honours?

To homages when they came from friends. It was then like a family celebration. He was utterly indifferent to official honours, elaborate funerals and the like. That's why he didn't want a lot of people attending his funeral: only his son, his son's girlfriend, the old servant who was with us, and my father-in-law's secretary who had been with us since she was fifteen. Darius died on a Saturday and we were supposed to take him from Geneva to Aix-en-Provence for his funeral on the Tuesday, to be buried by the side of his parents. My idea was that the news wouldn't be released until after the funeral. But on the Monday morning I received telegrams of condolence from America, so obviously word had got out. I was very worried because there was a music festival in Aix at that moment, and a lot of curious people coming to watch was exactly what I didn't want. So I called the mayor, who had an idea that could only belong to the south of France. 'Oh, it's very easy,' he said, 'we'll announce the funeral for Wednesday.' 'But have we the right to do that?' I asked. 'Certainly,' he said, 'and in the Tuesday night's papers we'll say we made a mistake, and that the funeral had unfortunately already taken place.' I said 'Amen!'

Since the death of Milhaud you have been – and are still – extraordinarily busy looking after Milhaud's musical legacy, not least in giving generously of your time to students and musicologists. Has this been a period for you personally of rediscovering his music?

I would not say rediscovering. But through being led to study some works very closely with certain performers, I have got to know some pieces much better than before, and I am struck by the fact that in Darius's music there are always new details to be discovered. Perhaps as I have devoted my life so much to poetry and drama, I notice this especially in his songs. The relationship between text and music in even his earliest songs is extraordinarily intimate and full of subtle expression.

The title of Milhaud's autobiography is _My Happy Life_. Would you say the same of your own life?

Darius and I lived together in absolutely harmonious coexistence without the slightest cloud for more than fifty years. We never had any arguments and never a moment of boredom. Milhaud once said to me it was because he always said 'yes' to me. I replied that I could then always change my mind and say 'no'. It is true that when you love someone, a 'no' is heard as a 'yes'!

I once asked a psychologist, 'What would you do with a patient of yours who from the age of seventeen to ninety devoted herself entirely to one man?'. 'I would lock her up', he replied.

30. Madeleine, Paris, 1995, with Mitsou

Index

Note: Works by Darius Milhaud are indexed alphabetically; others will be found under the name of their creator.

Numbers in **bold** refer to illustrations.